Outdoor Playhouses & Toys

Outdoor Playhouses & Toys

The Staff of Workbench Magazine

Sterling Publishing Co., Inc.   New York

Library of Congress Cataloging-in-Publication Data

Main entry under title:
Outdoor playhouses & toys.

Includes index.
1. Wooden toy making. 2. Playhouses, Children's.
I. Workbench. II. Title: Outdoor playhouses and toys.
TT174.5.W6098 1985 684′.08 84-26764
ISBN 0-8069-6208-9 (pbk.)

Copyright © 1985 by Modern Handcraft, Inc.
Published in 1985 by Sterling Publishing Co., Inc.
387 Park Avenue South, New York, N.Y. 10016
Originally published under the titles "The Workbench
Treasury of Wooden Toy Projects" and "The Workbench
Treasury of Outdoor Toys and Playhouses" © 1982 and
1983, respectively, by Modern Handcraft, Inc.
Distributed in Canada by Sterling Publishing
℅ Canadian Manda Group, P.O. Box 920, Station U
Toronto, Ontario, Canada M8Z 5P9
Distributed in Great Britain and Europe by Cassell PLC
Artillery House, Artillery Row, London SW1P 1RT, England
Distributed in Australia by Capricorn Ltd.
P.O. Box 665, Lane Cove, NSW 2066
Manufactured in the United States of America

Contents

Introduction

The wonderful world of outdoor playhouses and toys is now open to the home craftsman. With these plans you can not only build lasting playthings that will long be appreciated, but also enjoy hours of crafting and exercise. Making these toys will enable you to demonstrate your expertise and maybe even satisfy a creative urge. And, of course, letting a child help construct the toy will increase his or her enjoyment of it.

This book is much more than a mere collection of mechanical drawings. Chosen from nearly a quarter century of the most popular *Workbench* magazine outdoor projects, this selection typifies the magazine's rigid criteria for children's playthings: they must be safe, fun, and educational.

Above all, *Workbench* toys must be child-safe. Never take shortcuts or substitute unsafe materials that might in any way be dangerous to a child. Sharp edges, slivery or splintery wood, protruding hardware, poisonous lead-based paints, and glass or shatterable plastics, are all avoided in *Workbench* toy plans.

Toys must be fun for those who play with them. Each of these projects was actually built by a *Workbench* reader, each was fun-tested with children, and each has successfully withstood this rugged proving ground.

Because child's play is educational, these toys are designed to aid in teaching children wholesome pursuits befitting their age.

We have included only those projects that can be homemade. In some instances, we suggest alternatives to basic plans, and alternatives by readers are encouraged. Originality of design distinguishes these playtime favorites from all others. Some are unique and may open a whole new world of fun for today's children. Some are heirlooms with only a fresh coat of paint to mark the passing years.

We have attempted to simplify plans, keep explanations short and to the point, and translate technical terms into conversational language wherever possible. Please note that in some cases a drawing has been reproduced on a grid because it was designed to ac-

commodate a particular youngster or a specific application. To enlarge the book's drawing, first determine how much larger you want it to be: 10 percent, 25 percent, 50 percent. Then draw a grid on paper or stock and increase the size of the squares accordingly. For example, if the book has 1-in. squares and you want to increase the size by 25 percent, make your grid squares 1¼ in. Finally, draw a portion of the book's pattern in the new grid one square at a time, making the line through the new square correspond directly to the line running through the book's square.

If you are unsure what scale to use, measure the critical dimension for the project: a child's leg, arm, or height. Be sure to allow for the child's rapid growth. Drawings on grids make it easier to adapt plans to the actual dimensions of the stock you will be using.

One final note: hardwoods, fine tools, and special hardware are not always available locally. Thousands of home craftsmen have found that regular advertisers in *Workbench* are dependable sources for these supplies.

Playground set

Swings, slides and teeter-totters are always favorite outdoor toys with children. If you're not impressed with the mass-produced versions, build your own set out of wood. Not only will it blend better with your home and yard, but it will provide years of fun for your children.

This set, which can be built in a couple of weekends, was constructed of redwood, but other strong, weather-resistant woods are suitable. Another swing and teeter-totter may be added by extending the length.

Select a fairly level spot and dig holes for the four corner posts. Plan to assemble the posts and braces when you have some help to hold them. Place the assembled unit on a level surface such as a driveway and with your helper to steady it, use a level to plumb the posts and level the cross braces. Attach temporary braces, set the unit in the holes, level it again and pour the concrete. Leave about 2 in. on top to fill with dirt.

Next, build the slide catwalk frame, fasten the cleats inside it and nail the flooring to the cleats. Level the catwalk and fasten it to the posts with lag screws. Two of the catwalk support posts make up the ladder sides. Dowels are fitted in holes in the supports for rungs. Drive screws into the rungs from the back of the posts.

Attach the catwalk rails to the catwalk supports with lag screws through the half-lap joints. Notice that the catwalk only comes to the center of the support posts, which enables you to fasten the slide to

both the catwalk and support posts.

To build the slide, nail the cleats to the cross supports first, then nail the side rails to this assembly. Cut the end cleats and rails to the profiles shown in the drawing, assemble the landing section and attach it to the slide. With the wooden portion of the slide assembled, clamp the upper end to the catwalk and prop up the lower end to the desired height. Raising the bottom end will slow the child's sliding speed, while lowering it will increase the speed.

When you have determined the height of the slide, fasten the support bar between the two posts, dig your holes and set the posts in concrete. When the concrete has set, nail the slide to the bottom support, drive lag screws at the top.

You probably won't be able to get sheet metal for the slide in lengths longer than 8 ft., so start at the top allowing about 4 in. overlap onto the catwalk. Cut a piece for the rest of the slide allowing enough extra to bend the metal over the end and fasten it to the bottom cross support. The top piece should overlap the bottom one slightly for the smoothest surface. Nail the metal to the cleats with galvanized nails.

Cut the swing support, notch it and drill holes for the swing eyebolts. After attaching the support with lag screws, cut out the swing seats, drill holes for eyebolts and attach the chains.

Drill the holes for the teeter-totter support and "monkey bar." Drill through the outside support

post, but only halfway through the main support. Cut the pipes short enough to drive a lag screw into the outside post to retain them. Level the pipes and attach the teeter-totter board with U-bolts.

The companion sandbox is a must in every playground ensemble. It is a simple project with the plan shown. Materials for it are not included below.

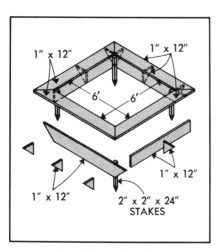

SANDBOX PLAN

1" x 12"
1" x 12"
6' 6'
1" x 12"
1" x 12"
2" x 2" x 24" STAKES

MATERIALS LIST

A, Main uprights, 4 x 4 x 9' (4)
B, Slide supports and ladder, 2 x 2 x 105-1/4" (3)
C, Top braces, 2 x 4 x 4' (4)
D, Swing support, 4 x 4 x 4' (1)
E, Teeter-totter post, 4 x 4 x 4' (1)
F, Slide support post, 2 x 4 x 25" (2)
G, Slide support, 2 x 4 x 15-1/2" (1)
H, Teeter-totter, 2 x 12 x 14' (1)
I, Ladder rungs, 1" x 17-3/4" dowels (5)
J, Hand rail, 2 x 2 x 18-3/4" (1)
K, Hand rail, 2 x 2 x 30-1/4" (1)
L, Slide, sheet metal, 14" x 122"
M, Slide rails, 1 x 4 x 9' (2)
N, Slide rails, 1 x 4 x 12" (2)
O, Catwalk frame rails, 1 x 4 x 47" (2)
P, Catwalk back, 1 x 4 x 14" (1)
Q, Catwalk bottom, 1 x 4 x 14" (13)
R, Slide dividers, 1 x 2 x 12-1/2" (6)
S, Catwalk bottom cleats, 1" x 1" x 47" (2)
T, Teeter-totter support, gas pipe, 1-1/2" x 3' (1)
U, Monkey bar, gas pipe, 1-1/2" x 44" (1)
V, Slide end cleats, 1" x 7" x 19" (2)
W, Slide cleats, 1" x 1-1/2" x 9' (2)

Ends of all exposed posts are tapered to provide runoff surface and prevent rotting of the post tops.

Teeter-totter is held in place by piece of pipe run through holes in support posts. Extra height holes are provided.

Suspend swing from 4 x 4 crossbar notched into main cross supports. Eyebolts are used to attach chain.

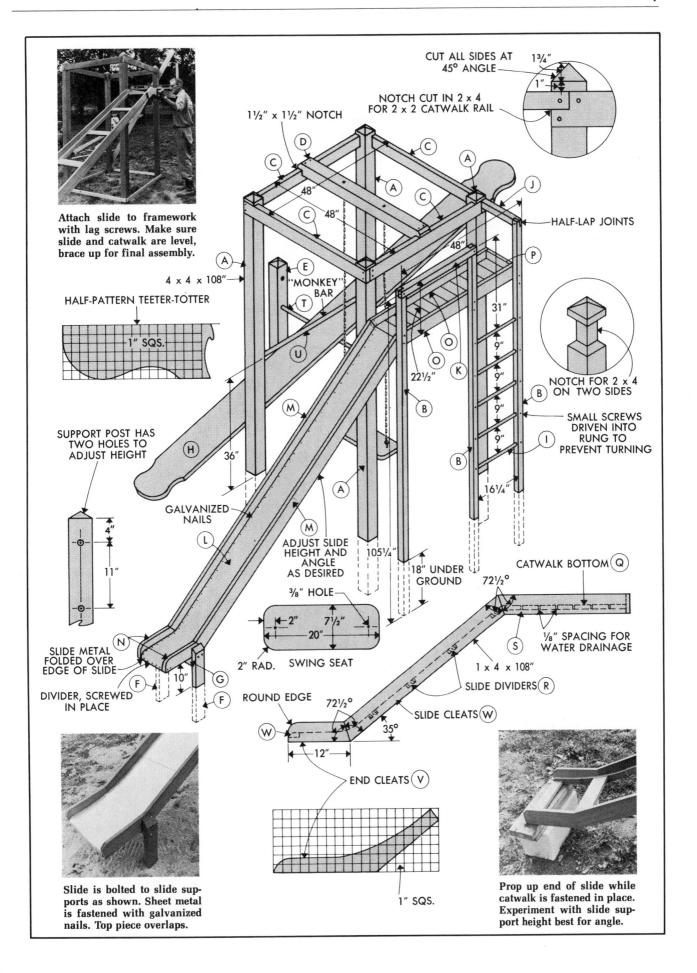

CUT ALL SIDES AT 45° ANGLE

1¾"

1"

NOTCH CUT IN 2 x 4 FOR 2 x 2 CATWALK RAIL

1½" x 1½" NOTCH

D

C

C

C

C

A

A

C

A

J

HALF-LAP JOINTS

48"

48"

48"

P

Attach slide to framework with lag screws. Make sure slide and catwalk are level, brace up for final assembly.

A

4 x 4 x 108"

E

"MONKEY" BAR

T

31"

9"

9"

9"

9"

NOTCH FOR 2 x 4 ON TWO SIDES

B

HALF-PATTERN TEETER-TOTTER

1" SQS.

U

O

O

K

22½"

B

SMALL SCREWS DRIVEN INTO RUNG TO PREVENT TURNING

M

B

I

SUPPORT POST HAS TWO HOLES TO ADJUST HEIGHT

H

36"

GALVANIZED NAILS

A

16¼"

4"

11"

L

M

ADJUST SLIDE HEIGHT AND ANGLE AS DESIRED

⅜" HOLE

105¼"

18" UNDER GROUND

CATWALK BOTTOM Q

72½"

⅛" SPACING FOR WATER DRAINAGE

S

N

2" 7½"

20"

SLIDE METAL FOLDED OVER EDGE OF SLIDE

F

10"

G

2" RAD.   SWING SEAT

1 x 4 x 108"

SLIDE DIVIDERS R

DIVIDER, SCREWED IN PLACE

F

ROUND EDGE

72½°

SLIDE CLEATS W

W

35°

12"

END CLEATS V

Slide is bolted to slide supports as shown. Sheet metal is fastened with galvanized nails. Top piece overlaps.

1" SQS.

Prop up end of slide while catwalk is fastened in place. Experiment with slide support height best for angle.

Self-covering sandbox

Digging in the sand is one of the pleasures of childhood, and a sandbox in the backyard will accommodate this childhood urge in the cleanest possible manner. Purchased sandboxes too often are not large enough, are flimsy in construction and cannot be covered properly. This latter factor is a particularly serious drawback, as it is important to keep leaves, animals and the like out of play sand.

This unique sandbox is strongly made from construction-grade fir lumber and white pine shelving and sheathing. The sandbox is big enough for a number of youngsters to play in, and strong enough to stand up under their rough-housing. When folded back, the top serves as a windbreak and a seat back. In the folded down position, the cover provides plenty of protection for the sandbox, and is rugged enough to permit children to

sit and climb on it.

The sides of the cover are cut from a single piece of lumber, and the simple trick shown assures accurate angles. Nail the longer pieces of 2 in. stock to the shorter with 16d common nails, and use finishing nails for the 1 in. lumber and sheathing. When fastening the three 2 x 4s that are used for bottom supports, drill three equally-spaced holes in the bottoms of the two outside members, going about halfway through the stock. Drive 16d nails through these holes, using a punch to set them snugly into the 2 in. stock sides.

Bevel the ends of the bottom support pieces and treat them with wood preservative. Note that the center support is attached by nailing through the bottom of the box. The completed sandbox should be painted or stained.

MATERIALS LIST

1 — Fir 2 x 8, 16'; cut 2 pcs. 51-1/4", 2 pcs. 44-1/2"
1 — Fir 2 x 4, 12'; cut 3 pcs. 46" with diagonal ends
1 — White pine 1 x 12, 9'; cut 2 pcs. 7-5/8" x 47-3/4", 2 pcs. 2" x 51-1/4"
1 — White pine 1 x 8, 6'; cut 2 pcs. 31-1/2", 2 pcs. 20"
8 — 1 x 6 T&G sheathing, 8'; cut 8 pcs. 49-3/4", 8 pcs. 39-1/4"
1 — 1 x 6 T&G sheathing, 16'; cut 3 pcs. 49-3/4", 1 pc. 39-1/4"
3 prs. galv. butt hinges, 3" x 4"
1 lb. 8d galv. or alum. finishing nails
1 lb. 6d galv. or alum. finishing nails
1 lb. 16d galv. or alum. common nails
Wood preservative
Paint (including undercoat) or penetrating pigmented sealer

Handsaw, portable electric or table saw can be used to cut lumber for sandbox. If a portable electric saw is used, a protractor or other device should be employed to assure accurate right angle cuts.

If you have no taper jig for your saw try this stunt: nail a piece of stock with one edge parallel to the line to be cut, and an inch or two away. Hold the stock against the rip fence as indicated.

Assemble box frame with 16d galvanized or aluminum nails. Set shorter pieces inside with edges flush with edges of seat. Use seat as guide or set 6 in. in from ends.

After nailing on seats, turn box over and nail T&G sheathing to bottom. Tongue on first strip is ripped off, board projects over edge of frame just 5/8 in. Use 8d nails here.

Drill three equally-spaced holes, slightly larger than heads of 16d nails, halfway through edge of two of the bottom-support pieces. Drive 16d nails into frame of box, with aid of punch.

Rip one of the pieces of sheathing with angled edge, nail it to peak of shorter pair of sides of the top. Strip with tongue goes on edge of longer pair of sides.

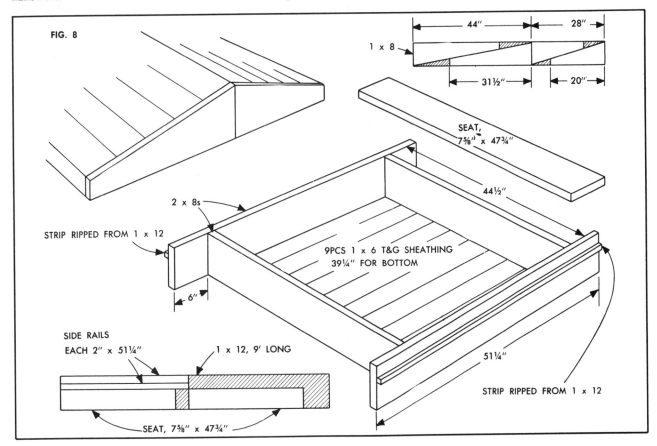

FIG. 8

1 x 8

44″   28″

31½″   20″

SEAT, 7⅝″ x 47¾″

44½″

2 x 8s

STRIP RIPPED FROM 1 x 12

9PCS 1 x 6 T&G SHEATHING 39¼″ FOR BOTTOM

6″

51¼″

STRIP RIPPED FROM 1 x 12

SIDE RAILS EACH 2″ x 51¼″

1 x 12, 9′ LONG

SEAT, 7⅝″ x 47¾″

Stick horse

This popular toy is made by first enlarging the squared drawing to make a pattern of the horse head. If you are a bit handy with a pencil, there is no reason why the head can't be that of a fierce dragon.

The stick will vary in diameter and length according to the height of the child. Don't forget to consult with the child about this. He or she might prefer a dragon to tower above them, while a gentle pony would have a head just below that of the child.

While a dowel is indicated in the drawing, there is no reason that an old broom or mop handle can't be used. The original stick animals were created that way and they still can be today.

Round the bottom end so it drags more easily, and if the youngster might occasionally gallop right into the house, a crutch tip fitted to the bottom end could minimize scuffing floors.

Harness on the horse would be black or brown, while the horse itself can be one of many colors. The child might have a favorite like a palomino or an appaloosa and you can paint the horse to suit. Dragons usually are green.

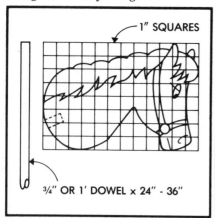

1" SQUARES

¾" OR 1' DOWEL × 24" - 36"

Little red wagon

One of the most popular of all toys for youngsters is a wagon. Because red was the most popular color, even when some models were made of metal, the term "little red wagon" has become almost the standard description of these vehicles.

When you build such a wagon the main factor is strength. Youngsters will use the wagon for hauling each other, rocks, dirt, groceries and anything else that will fit. The wagon also will be expected to go up and down curbs, over rocks and through muddy fields. The wagon has to be rugged.

Hardwood is used for constructing the wagon, and for the one shown, oak was chosen.

The first step is to enlarge the squared drawings for the front and rear axle carriers, and for the yokes to which the handle is fastened. Note that braces are attached to each end of each axle, and the grain for the braces runs vertically, rather than horizontally as for the carriers.

This strengthens the axles, and the braces are attached with glue. Since the wagon often will be left out in the weather, it's a good idea

to use waterproof glue. It also would add strength to the assembly if you drove a few screws through the braces into the axle carriers.

The next step is to drill the 1/2 in. holes through the axle carriers to accept the steel rods used for the axles. While threaded rod was used for the wagon shown, with nuts and washers on the ends to hold the wheels, you might prefer an unthreaded rod. Holes for cotter keys are drilled near the ends of the rods to hold on the wheels.

When cotter keys are used, the wheels should be the type with snap on caps that cover the ends of the axles when the wheels are in place. This would prevent cutting or bruising legs of active youngsters.

At this point, install the wheels to make sure they fit properly. If you use threaded rod, cut off any excess rod that projects. Remove the wheels and proceed with the rest of the assembly.

Cut a 6 in. disk of hardwood 3/4 in. thick (all stock used is 3/4 in. thick) and glue and screw it to the top of the front axle carrier. Make sure that it projects slightly above the axle carrier, which it will if the notch in the carrier is 5/8 in. as indicated. Also glue and screw the two handle yokes to the front of the carrier, spaced to allow the handle, with a washer on each side, to pivot easily between them. Drill the 1/2 in. hole through the disc and the axle carrier for the pivot bolt.

Next, make the wagon bed, assembling it with glue and No. 8 x 1-1/4 in. flathead wood screws. Fit the screws in counterbored holes and cover them with wooden plugs glued in place.

The bottom of the wagon bed is attached to the sides and ends with flathead wood screws in countersunk holes. The screws on the underside of the bed do not need to be covered with wooden plugs. Just be sure the screw heads are recessed into the bottom pieces.

Glue and screw the 3 x 14-1/2 in. bolt carrier to the top of the bed between the sides and front, then drill the hole for the pivot bolt. Be sure it is centered in both directions.

Turn the bed upside down and attach the rear axle by means of the notched cleat that first is glued and screwed to the back of the axle carrier. Also attach the two brackets (Detail A). Fasten them by driving screws through the axle carrier and down through the bed. Other screws are driven down through the bed into the axle carrier and the notched cleat.

The front axle is fitted to the bed next. Before doing this you might want to fasten a piece of sheet metal to the bottom of the bed over the area that will be contacted by the 6 in. axle disc. The metal will prevent wear on the bottom of the bed.

Join the front axle assembly to the bed with the 1/2 in. bolt. The metal brace has one end bolted to the underside of the bed, the other fits on the bottom of the pivot bolt. The brace should fit snugly on the pivot bolt, but loosely enough so the front axle pivots freely.

One method of doing this is to adjust the nut tightly enough so the axle moves freely, then to upset the threads of the bolt so the nut will not loosen.

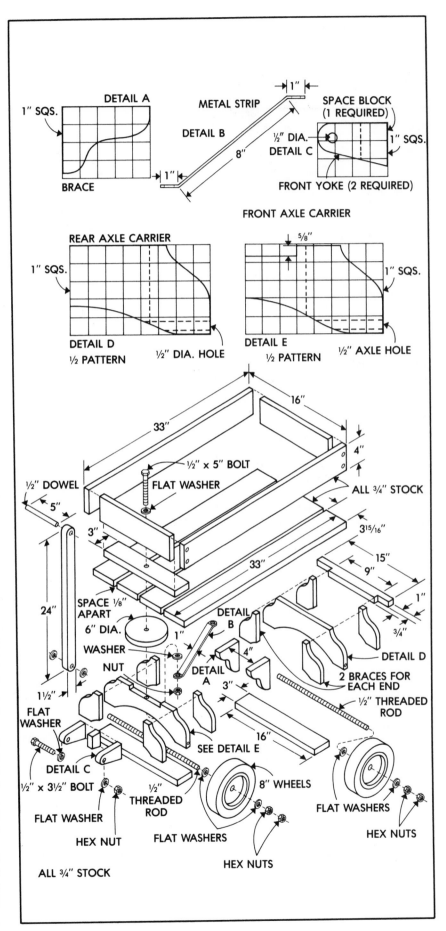

Wheelbarrow

Start by enlarging the squared drawing to make a pattern for the sides. Cut the sides to shape and round and sand the curved edges.

Cut the bottom and front to size and join to the sides with glue and No. 8 x 1-1/4 in. flathead wood screws. Fit the screws in counterbored holes and cover with wooden plugs. Sand the completed wheelbarrow body.

Cut the handles to size from 5/4 stock (1-1/4 in.) and shape the angles on the front ends. Drill for the dowel axle. Round all edges and corners on the ends of the handles, then round at least 4 in. of each handle where it is gripped.

The wheel is made by cutting a disk from 5/4 stock a bit larger than the 6-1/2 in. diameter indicated. The cut out wheel then is fitted on a 1/2 in. bolt and chucked in a drill press or drill motor and rotated and sanded to true it up and round the edges.

Cut the legs and glue and screw them to the undersides of the handles. Fit the wheel between the handles and drive a 1/2 in. dowel through the handles and wheel. Cut off any projection of the dowel and sand smooth. Next, drive a 1-1/4 in. wood screw from the underside of each handle so it enters the dowel axle and holds it in place.

Turn the body upside down and position the handles so the front of the body is 1 in. from the wheel. Center the rear end of the body on the handles.

Drive screws down through the bottom of the body into the handles.

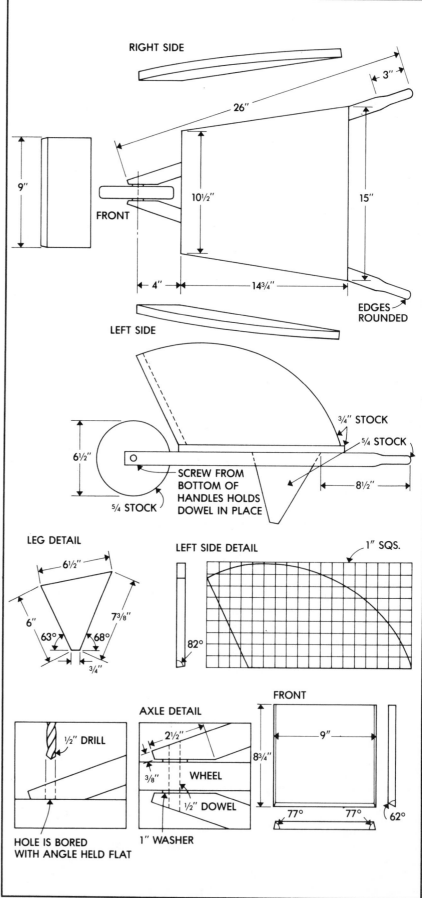

Kiddy car

This kiddy car is dimensioned for a fairly good sized youngster, but can be scaled down for a smaller tot.

Start by enlarging the two squared drawings to make patterns for the seat and the support brackets for the rear axle.

Cut the seat and brackets to size and shape. Hardwood is recommended.

Smooth and round all edges of the seat, and drill the hole for the steering column that is sized to accept a 7 in. length of 3/4 in. thin wall conduit. You could replace this with a short length of 1/2 in. steel pipe, but the dowel that fits in the lower end would be 1/2 in. rather than the 3/4 in. shown in the drawing.

Glue the reinforcements to the axle brackets, then drill the 3/4 in. hole in each bracket when the waterproof glue sets. The reinforcements are positioned so their grain is at right angles to the grain of the axle brackets.

Cut the pieces for the yoke that holds the front wheel and assemble with glue and flathead screws. The disc at the bottom of the dowel in the steering column assembly should be as round as possible.

Drill the 1-1/2 x 1-1/2 x 5 in. handle block for the dowels and tubing and the locking bolt, then insert the tubing and drill through the block and tubing for the nut and bolt.

Slide the handle/column through the seat and slip in the yoke assembly. Drill through the tubing and yoke dowel and insert the nut and bolt.

Glue the dowel handles into the handle block.

The axles can be threaded rod as indicated, with washers and nuts to hold on the wheels, or better still, plain rod can be used, with holes drilled near the ends for cotter keys. Cover the axle ends with some sort of "hub cap," such as cups turned from wood so youngsters do not injure their legs.

Wheels can be discs cut from wood, or you can use purchased wheels, of the type sold as replacements for lawn and garden equipment.

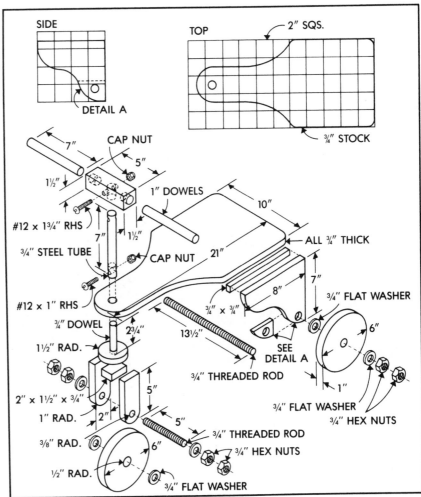

Pedal car racer

Inspired by the Formula cars that run the Grand Prix circuit, this car has been reduced to the basics so there are no compound curves in the bodywork.

Start construction by making a pattern for the sides by enlarging the squared drawing. Cut the two sides from 1/2 in. plywood with the good side out.

Cleats cut from 1 in. softwood are glued and screwed to the inner surfaces of the sides, flush with upper edges. Hardwood cleats for supporting the pillow block bearings for the rear axle are glued and screwed in position, as indicated.

The front of the body is joined by the front axle cleat, which first is grooved as indicated. Crosspieces at the top of the body are about 15-1/2 in. long, which should be the distance between the 1/2 in. grooves in the axle cleat less twice the thickness of the upper cleats inside the body. Cleats at the rear part of the body should be the same length.

The crank support is glued and screwed to the center groove in the front axle cleat at the forward end, while the back end is supported on two cleats glued and screwed under the seat.

To make the pedal drive you first weld, or have welded, a short length of 1/2 in. black iron pipe to a piece of steel angle. Slot the angle as indicated, to permit tightening or loosening the belt. Drill a hole near the center of the pipe and tap for a grease fitting.

The crank can be made in two ways: First, bend a Z shape which will be one arm with the pedal extension and the portion that goes through the pipe. Install the shaft collars and pulley loosely, then weld on to this bent crank the other portion of the crank. Center the crank, tighten the collars and lubricate.

The second method is to insert the rod in the crank support, heat the rod at the bending points and bend the crank to shape.

Install the rear bearings and axle with pulley. Align front and rear pulleys, install the belt and tighten. Finally, install the steering assembly and paint.

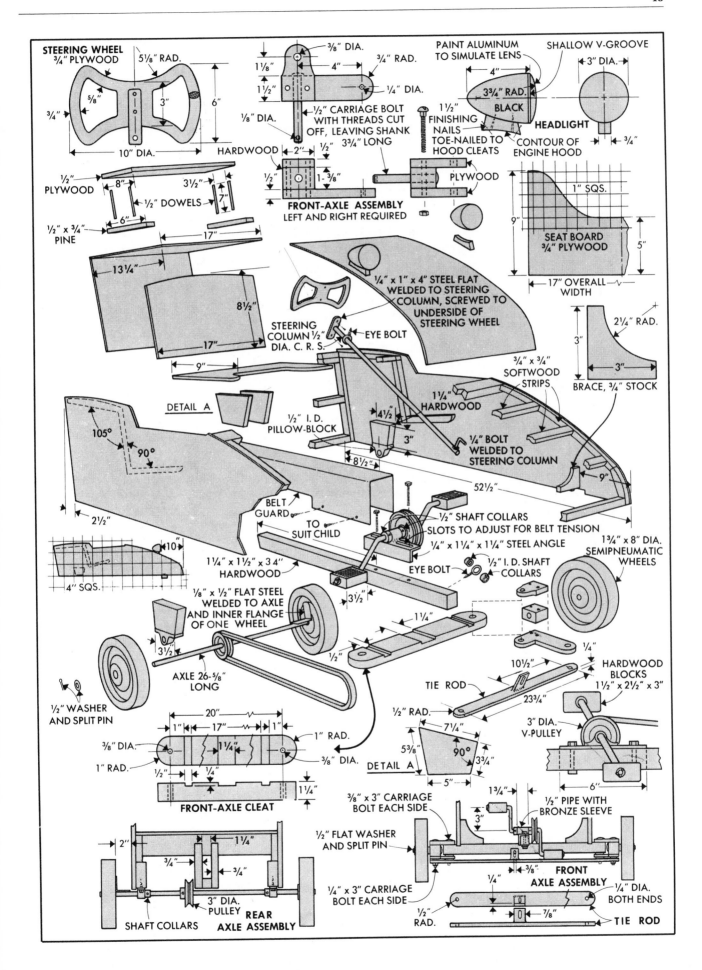

STEERING WHEEL
¾" PLYWOOD
5⅛" RAD.
⅝"
¾"
3"
6"
10" DIA.

⅜" DIA.
1⅛"
1½"
4"
¾" RAD.
¼" DIA.
⅛" DIA.
½" CARRIAGE BOLT
WITH THREADS CUT
OFF, LEAVING SHANK
3¾" LONG

PAINT ALUMINUM
TO SIMULATE LENS
SHALLOW V-GROOVE
3" DIA.
4"
3¾" RAD.
BLACK
HEADLIGHT
¾"
CONTOUR OF
ENGINE HOOD

1½" FINISHING
NAILS
TOE-NAILED TO
HOOD CLEATS

½" PLYWOOD
8"
3½"
7"
½" DOWELS
6"
½" x ¾" PINE
17"
13¼"
8½"
17"
9"

HARDWOOD
2"
½"
1-⅜"
PLYWOOD
FRONT-AXLE ASSEMBLY
LEFT AND RIGHT REQUIRED

1" SQS.
9"
SEAT BOARD
¾" PLYWOOD
5"
17" OVERALL WIDTH

¼" x 1" x 4" STEEL FLAT
WELDED TO STEERING
COLUMN, SCREWED TO
UNDERSIDE OF
STEERING WHEEL

STEERING
COLUMN ½"
DIA. C. R. S.
EYE BOLT

¾" x ¾"
SOFTWOOD
STRIPS

2¼" RAD.
3"
3"
BRACE, ¾" STOCK

DETAIL A
105°
90°
½" I. D.
PILLOW-BLOCK
1¼"
HARDWOOD
4½"
3"
8½"
¼" BOLT
WELDED TO
STEERING COLUMN
52½"
9"

2½"
10"
4" SQS.
BELT GUARD
TO SUIT CHILD
1¼" x 1½" x 3 4"
HARDWOOD
½" SHAFT COLLARS
SLOTS TO ADJUST FOR BELT TENSION
¼" x 1¼" x 1¼" STEEL ANGLE
EYE BOLT
½" I. D. SHAFT COLLARS
1¾" x 8" DIA.
SEMIPNEUMATIC
WHEELS

⅛" x ½" FLAT STEEL
WELDED TO AXLE
AND INNER FLANGE
OF ONE WHEEL
3½"
3½"
½"
1¼"
AXLE 26-⅝" LONG

½" WASHER
AND SPLIT PIN

20"
1"
17"
1"
1" RAD.
⅜" DIA.
1¼"
1" RAD.
⅜" DIA.
½"
¼"
FRONT-AXLE CLEAT
1¼"

TIE ROD
10½"
½" RAD.
23¾"
7¼"
5⅜"
90°
3¾"
DETAIL A
5"
¼"
HARDWOOD BLOCKS
1½" x 2½" x 3"
3" DIA. V-PULLEY
6"

3" DIA.
PULLEY
REAR
AXLE ASSEMBLY
SHAFT COLLARS
2"
1¼"
¾"
¾"

⅜" x 3" CARRIAGE
BOLT EACH SIDE
½" FLAT WASHER
AND SPLIT PIN
¼" x 3" CARRIAGE
BOLT EACH SIDE
1¾"
3"
½" PIPE WITH
BRONZE SLEEVE
FRONT
AXLE ASSEMBLY
¼"
⅜"
¼" DIA.
BOTH ENDS
½" RAD.
⅞"
TIE ROD

Skate board scooter

Remember the old-fashioned scooters that were made from a fruit box, a length of 2 x 4 and the wheels from a roller skate? This updated version combines the old with the new by replacing the conventional base and undercarriage with a modern skateboard. Safer than a skateboard for small fry, and capable of providing plenty of fun, this scooter is designed to resemble a truck for added appeal.

Skateboard metal wheels will last longer than composition wheels, but the latter are recommended because they are less likely to skid and cause spills.

Begin construction by cutting the floor from 3/4 in. exterior grade plywood. Notches are cut in the back end of the floor to allow for attachment of the dashboard. The floor is fastened to the skateboard with flathead wood screws.

Cut the handle uprights from 1 in. hardwood and attach to a 1 in. dowel with stove bolts. Be sure no rough edges of the bolts are left to cut small hands. Three holes are bored in each upright to permit screwing it to the dashboard assembly. Cut the dashboard from 3/4 in. exterior grade plywood to the size and shape shown. Round the corners to prevent injury.

Cut and fasten the engine wall cleats to the dashboard with glue and screws. The engine walls are then cut to size and tack nailed in place over the engine wall cleats. It is easier to cut the parts to size and shape and dry fit them, then disassemble and paint each piece individually.

When all joints match, glue and screw in place over the engine wall cleats and up against the dashboard. Cut the front panel to shape and fasten with finishing nails or screws to the front edges of the engine walls. A pattern can be made for the front panel by marking around the outside of the assembled engine walls. The front panel is outlined with trim and a trim panel is fastened over it, making the grill. Grill bars and a bumper are cut from solid stock and added to the front panel for more realism. The dashboard assembly is fitted over the floor and attached with screws into the edges of the floor. Then the handle uprights are attached with screws into the dashboard. Make sure none of the screws protrude.

It won't take youngsters long to learn how to balance the scooter and make turns by leaning in the direction they wish to go.

MATERIALS LIST

Skateboard (bought or made) (1)
Dashboard, 3/4″ x 13″ x 14″, exterior grade plywood (1)
Wall cleats, 7/8″ x 1″ x 30″, solid stock (1)
Front panel, 1/4″ x 11-1/4″ x 11-1/4″, plywood (1)
Engine walls, 1/2″ x 5″ x 30″, solid stock (1)
Panel trim, 1/4″ x 1-1/4″ x 10-3/4″, plywood (1)
Wall trim, 1/2″ x 1-1/2″ x 36″, solid stock (1)
Grill bars, 1/4″ x 1/2″ x 6-1/2″, solid stock (5)
Bumper, 5/8″ x 1″ x 13″, solid stock (1)
Handle uprights, 3/4″ x 1″ x 23″, hardwood (2)
Handle, 1″ dowel x 14″ (1)
Floor, 3/4″ x 6-1/4″ x 10-1/4″, exterior grade plywood (1)

Prancing ponies teeter-totter

The ponies on the sides of the seats keep little riders in place laterally, and a dowel handle provides a gripping bar up front.

Construction begins with the rocker arms that are cut from 3/4 in. plywood. If you draw the patterns side by side, you need only a width of slightly more than 24 in. and the full length of an 8 ft. sheet.

Two sets of cross members are fitted between the rocker arms. The two at the center are cut from 1-1/4 in. stock and fastened with screws and waterproof glue. The outside cross members are cut from 1 in. stock and glued and screwed in place.

Seats are attached near the ends of the arms, cleats underneath provide added support. To prevent the rocker arms from dropping to the ground and breaking the ponies' legs, there is a stop fitted under each seat.

The base is a rigid structure of 2 x 4s supporting two uprights cut from 2 x 8 stock. Cut the hardboard cover to size, cut the notches to fit over the uprights, then install with glue and nails.

Now, clamp the rocker arm assembly to the uprights and drill through the four members to accept the pivot rod that is a length of 1 in. black iron water pipe. Cut the pipe so it projects about 3/4 in. outside the rocker arms. Either thread the pipe and turn on caps, or drill the pipe to accept cotter keys.

Attach the ponies with the teeter-totter in the "down" position so there is about 1 in. clearance between the feet and the ground.

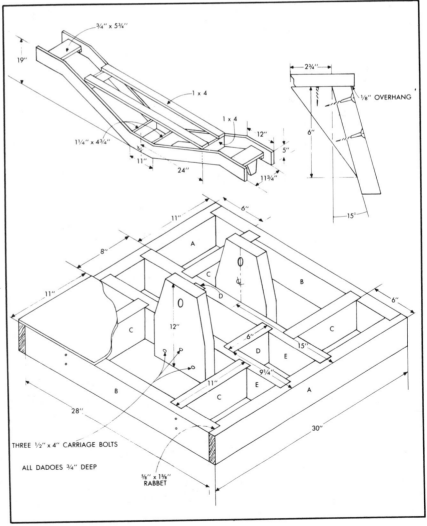

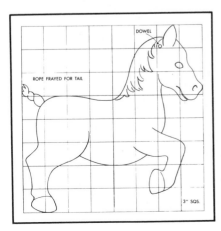

Old-fashioned lawn glider

Once a feature of almost every yard, lawn swings — often called gliders — are making a comeback because they are a cool and comfortable way to relax outdoors. The built-in table in a lawn swing provides a space for eating a light snack. Even containers of liquid can be placed on the table if the motion of the swing is kept down to a reasonable pace. Make either the adult or child size version of the old-fashioned glider; perhaps even both.

Start construction of either the junior size or the adult model by making the base track, Fig. 4. For the adult unit 2 x 4s are used, 1 x 2s for the junior size. Cut a rabbet in the two longer members of the frame to make them L shape tracks on which the wheels will run. The tracks must be parallel and the assembly square. As in Fig. 1, measure the diagonals of the frame to make sure they are the same; this will assure the frame being square. Assemble the frame with half lap joints, using waterproof glue and screws. The frame will be in direct contact with the ground, so treat the lumber with a wood preservative to assure long life.

The four wheels are turned on a lathe, Figs. 2 and 4. If your lathe does not have provision for outboard turning, the 16 in. wheels for the adult swing will require cutting on a bandsaw or jig saw. They are trued up by pivoting them against a sanding disk. Clamp a piece of plywood to the sander table, then use a headless nail as a pivot to turn the wheels against the disk to make them all the same size. Drill the holes as indicated to receive the dowels that connect them in pairs. Use a depth stop so all holes are of equal depth. The wheels then are glued to the dowels that are tapped into the holes. Make sure the wheels are absolutely parallel to each other in each pair. When you are sure, drive a finishing nail through the rims of the wheel and through the dowels. Dowels for the child's swing are 3/4 x 19-7/8 in., and are fitted in holes bored 5/16 in. deep in the wheel. The dowels for the adult's swing are a 1-1/2 in. diameter closet pole set in holes 3/4 in. deep. Determine the length of the 1-1/2 in. dowels by placing the wheels about 1/8 in. inside the edges of the base track, then measuring between them. Add twice 3/4 in. to this measurement for the holes.

The floor of the swing is next, Fig. 4. Note that on the adult floor the two center slats are cut flush with the side members. This is to clear the vertical table supports that are fitted inside on the adult swing. They are fitted outside on the child size unit, Fig. 6. The two center slats are spaced equidistant from the center of the floor, as indicated. Temporarily nail strips at the ends of the aligned side members to keep them in position until several slats have been glued and screwed in position. The finished floor now is fitted on the wheels, Fig. 3, and the rolling action checked.

The seats are next, Figs. 5 and 7. Note that the seats for the adult and child size gliders are similar, but that the slats on the back of the adult units are positioned vertically, those on the child size are horizontal.

Next to be assembled are the rocker frames, Fig. 5. Both sizes are similar, except that 1 x 2s are used for the small swing, 2 x 4s for the larger unit. Also, there are two horizontal braces on the child size frame, none on the adult unit. Half lap joints are used in the assembly of the frames.

The next step is to attach the seats to the frames, as shown in photo, Fig. 7. The lower edges of the seat frames that ride on the wheels must be absolutely parallel to the lower edges of the bottom frame members, and must be spaced from them less than the diameter of the wheels. This assures that the wheels will project below the lower edges of the bottom rocker frame member. Attach the frames to seats on the junior size with No. 8 round head screws 2 in. long. For assembling the senior size use 3/8 x 3-1/2 in. carriage bolts.

At this point you may wish to disassemble seats and rocker frames to permit complete painting. You can dry assemble the table to the frame, then remove it for painting also. When the paint is thoroughly dry, reassemble the swing and measure it for the canopy frame.

As indicated in Fig. 7, the uprights for the adult size canopy are 48 in., those for the junior swing are 30 in. These are screwed to the vertical members of the seat backs. For the adult size, measure between the uprights and cut and fit a length of 1 x 2. A canvas or plastic canopy then can be cut and sewn to fit. For the junior size, clamp a length of 1 x 2 to each upright, then angle them to the center of the swing. Determine the angle, cut the 1 x 2s, then splice them with a piece of 1/4 in. plywood. Cut and fit a canopy over this frame.

Fig. 1. The glider tracks must be accurately aligned and parallel. Measure diagonally to assure alignment.

Fig. 2. Wheels for the junior size glider are 8 in. in diameter, cut from 1 in. stock. For the 16 in. wheels, use 2 in. lumber.

Fig. 3. The floor and wheels assembly for both sizes is quite similar. The overall dimensions, of course, are varied to suit.

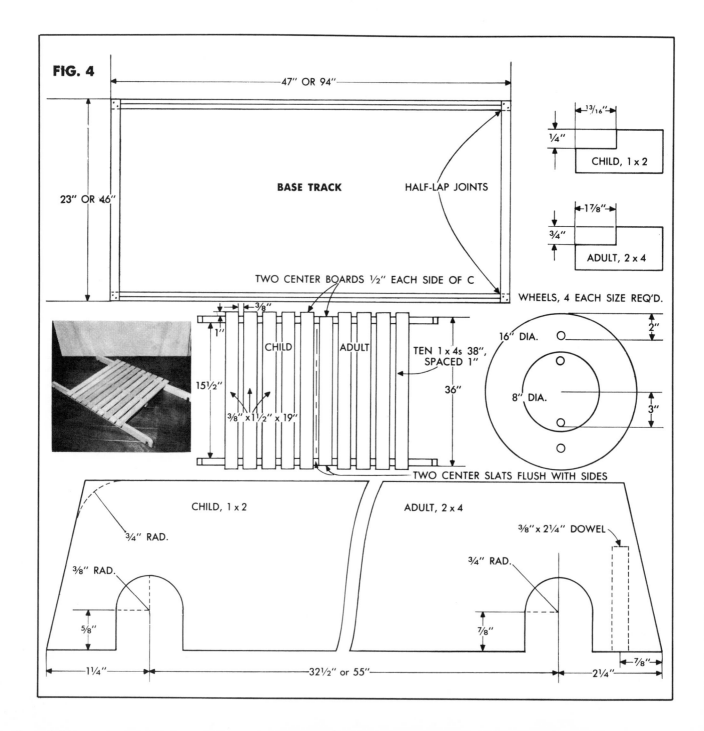

ROCKER FRAMES AND TABLES

FIG. 5

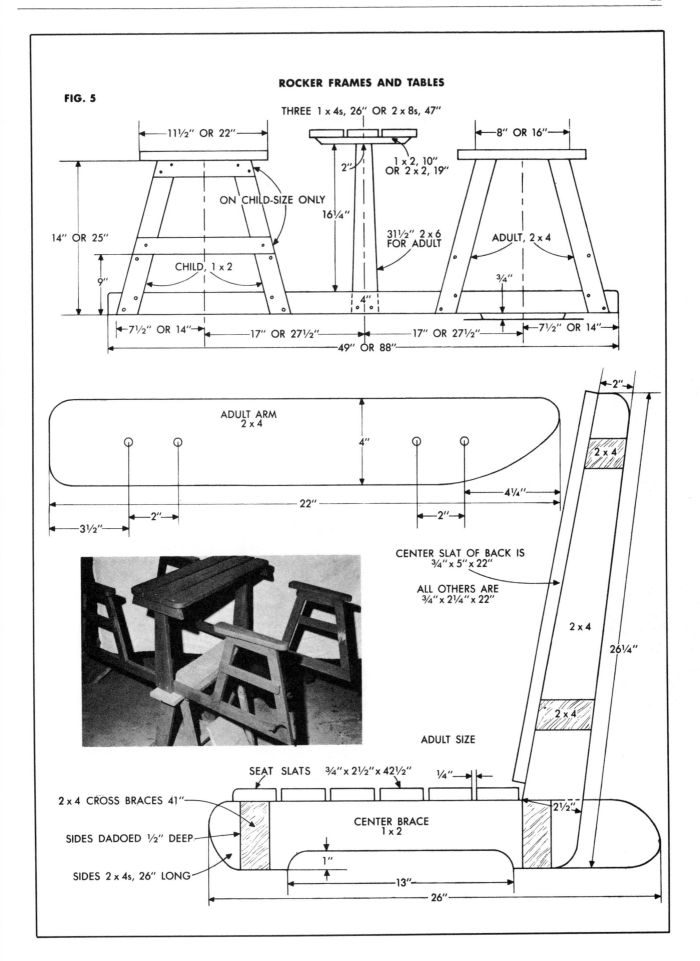

THREE 1 x 4s, 26" OR 2 x 8s, 47"

11½" OR 22"

8" OR 16"

2"

1 x 2, 10"
OR 2 x 2, 19"

ON CHILD-SIZE ONLY

16¼"

31½" 2 x 6
FOR ADULT

ADULT, 2 x 4

14" OR 25"

9"

CHILD, 1 x 2

¾"

4"

7½" OR 14"

17" OR 27½"

17" OR 27½"

7½" OR 14"

49" OR 88"

ADULT ARM
2 x 4

4"

4¼"

22"

2"

2"

3½"

CENTER SLAT OF BACK IS
¾" x 5" x 22"

ALL OTHERS ARE
¾" x 2¼" x 22"

2 x 4

2 x 4

2 x 4

2"

2 x 4

26¼"

ADULT SIZE

2½"

SEAT SLATS   ¾" x 2½" x 42½"   ¼"

2 x 4 CROSS BRACES 41"

CENTER BRACE
1 x 2

SIDES DADOED ½" DEEP

1"

SIDES 2 x 4s, 26" LONG

13"

26"

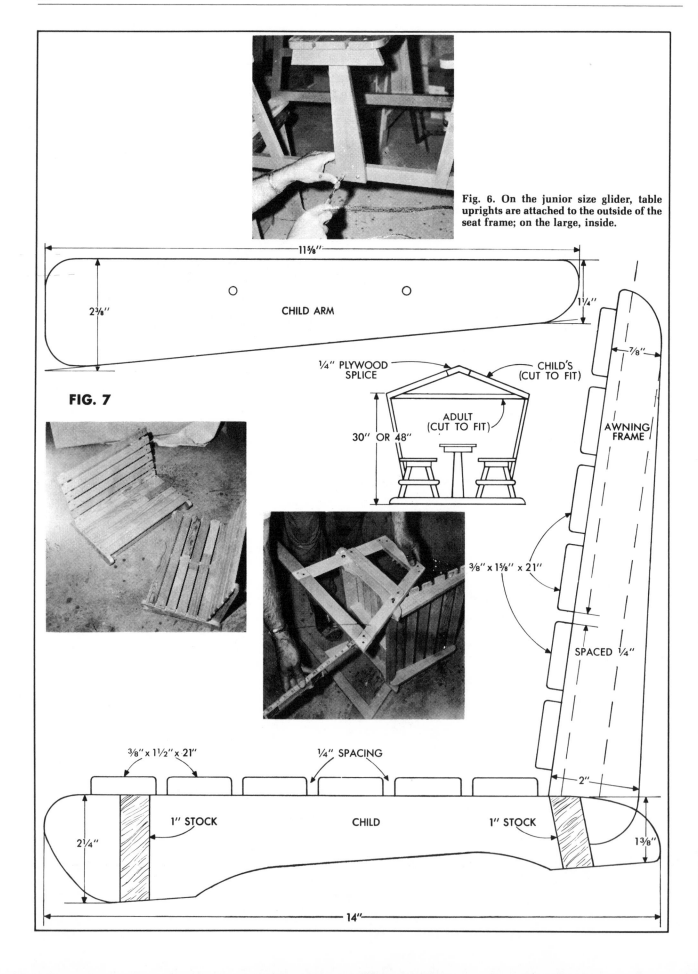

Fig. 6. On the junior size glider, table uprights are attached to the outside of the seat frame; on the large, inside.

11⅝"

2⅜"

CHILD ARM

1¼"

FIG. 7

¼" PLYWOOD SPLICE

CHILD'S (CUT TO FIT)

ADULT (CUT TO FIT)

30" OR 48"

⅞"

AWNING FRAME

⅜" x 1⅝" x 21"

SPACED ¼"

2"

⅜" x 1½" x 21"

¼" SPACING

1" STOCK

CHILD

1" STOCK

2¼"

1⅜"

14"

High-flying kites

To get your kite aloft in a minimum breeze, have it soar high and far, and maneuver it expertly in aerial games, depends as much on making a well engineered kite as on skill in flying it. These time-tested kite designs that require very little time and effort to construct are among the most rewarding.

The basic 4-point woodframe kite is the simplest type to make. The sticks can be cut with a power saw. Then saw kerfs at the ends of the sticks before assembling the frame. Corner blocks reinforce the joint. Use ordinary white glue. Cross the sticks at right angles at the exact midpoint of the lateral one. The lateral crosspiece faces the covering.

You can use nylon thread, twine or fishing line for the frame string. The size of this should be about the same as that of the kite string required, which varies with kite size as given in Table B on page 28. Bring the string through the saw kerfs and tie tautly without distorting the frame. If one of the sticks is warped, pull it straight with the frame string, looping it around the stick. Then secure the frame twine in each slot with glue. To attach the covering, lay the frame on it and stick strips of tape to both frame string and covering as shown.

A lateral crosspiece that is bowed toward the back gives the kite more stability. The crosspiece can be held in a bowed position with a cord knotted at its ends and held in place by the cross slots. Two knots at each end spaced 1/2 in. apart permit varying the amount of bow. A permanently bowed crosspiece, which is not held under tension with a cord, is better and less susceptible to breakage. To make one, use two sticks half the thickness of the single one. Coat the contacting surfaces with glue and arrange them in a jig, after which you clamp the pieces together with spring type clothespins spaced 2 or 3 in. apart. Let the glue dry overnight, then cut the kerfs and assemble the frame.

The table at bottom right gives thicknesses of square kite sticks made of spruce, white pine or basswood, for kites used in mild wind. To obtain more flexibility and minimize the possibility of breakage you can decrease the thickness and increase the width, keeping the cross-sectional area the same. For moderately heavy wind the cross-sectional area should be increased from 25 to 50 percent, but then the kite will be less suitable for mild wind. If heavier wood is used, the cross-sectional area should be reduced in inverse proportion to the increased weight as given in Table A on page 28. For example, if you used hickory (about twice the weight of basswood), the cross-sectional area is reduced by one-half.

WOOD FRAME 4-POINT KITE

GLUED

$\frac{1}{6}$ to $\frac{1}{4}$X

$\frac{5}{6}$X

USE SQUARE

90°

X

SINGLE SAW KERF AT TOP & BOTTOM

$\frac{1}{10}$ to $\frac{1}{6}$X

CROSSING SAW KERFS

BOARD

NAILS

JIG FOR PREFORMING BOW

$\frac{1}{2}$" TAPE

ADHERING THE COVERING TO FRAME STRING

APPROXIMATE THICKNESS OF SQUARE KITE STICKS*			
LENGTH	THICKNESS	LENGTH	THICKNESS
18	$\frac{3}{16}$	48	$\frac{3}{8}$
24	$\frac{1}{4}$	60	$\frac{1}{2}$
30	$\frac{1}{4}$	72	$\frac{5}{8}$
36	$\frac{5}{16}$		
*BASED ON USE OF STRAIGHT-GRAINED SPRUCE, WHITE PINE OR BASSWOOD			

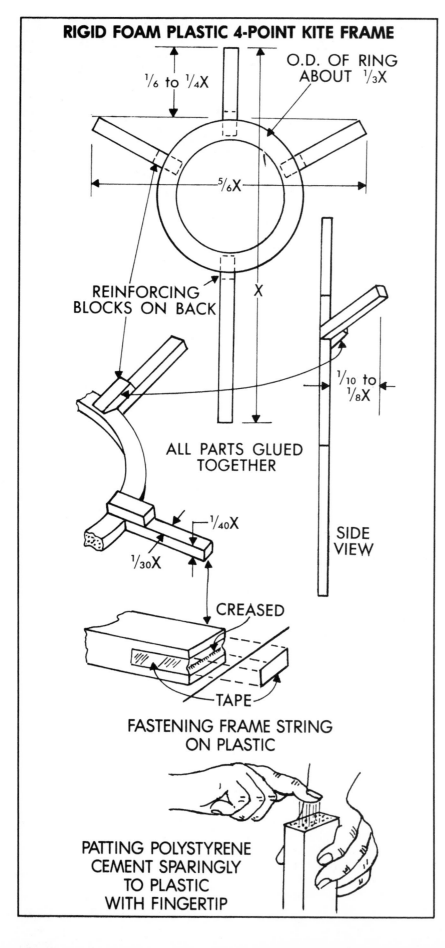

RIGID FOAM PLASTIC 4-POINT KITE FRAME

1/6 to 1/4X

O.D. OF RING ABOUT 1/3X

5/6X

X

REINFORCING BLOCKS ON BACK

ALL PARTS GLUED TOGETHER

1/10 to 1/8X

SIDE VIEW

1/40X

1/30X

CREASED

TAPE

FASTENING FRAME STRING ON PLASTIC

PATTING POLYSTYRENE CEMENT SPARINGLY TO PLASTIC WITH FINGERTIP

The diagrams at left show a frame constructed of rigid foam plastic. This material is available in blocks of various sizes and can be cut easily with a serrated bread knife or a fine-tooth saw. Precut rings such as for making wreaths are also available. Use of a ring maintains a relatively large area of flat surfaces besides providing maximum strength.

Use polystyrene cement to "weld" frame members together. Put the cement on sparingly with your finger on only one of the contacting surfaces. Then hold the pieces together under light pressure for about a minute.

Reinforcing blocks give added joint strength. These may be placed over joints, or fitted into corners. To produce the effect of a bowed crosspiece you can attach the side arms at an angle to slope backward, side view. The length of the straight frame pieces varies with both the kite size and the ring size.

You can cut rings on a scroll saw. Pivot the block to rotate on a slender nail driven into a 1/4 in. plywood plate having cleats along its edges to hold it on the saw table. The pivot must line up with the cutting edge of the blade and a line from pivot to cutting edge must be at right angles to the side of the blade. Cut the outer diameter first.

The frame string fits in shallow creases pressed into the ends of the sticks after protecting them with tape. When tying the string for tautness remove it from the stick nearest you and tie the knot so the string must be forced slightly to get it into the crease. Press a small piece of tape over the string to hold it in place. A covering of clear polyethylene plastic over the frame produces a striking effect, as only the dazzling white plastic foam frame is visible when the kite is aloft.

The method of making 6-point kites shown below is practically the same as for 4-point kites. One difference in wood frames is that a tiny pilot hole, about 1/64 in. diameter, is drilled for a slender brad or pin at the joint where the sticks cross. This serves as a pivot so the sticks can be adjusted after the frame string is in place. The adjustment consists of getting distance AB equal to CD and distance AF equal to DE. After making this adjustment, pry the joint loose enough to squeeze in some glue, then clamp the pieces together without disturbing the stick spacing. Insert two small reinforcing blocks, the same thickness as the sticks, under the lateral one and against the sides of the one under it, as detailed bottom left. The lateral one comes directly under the covering. It may be bowed to increase stability. On a plastic foam frame four of the arms are measured from the center of the ring. The lateral arms may be given a backward slope for increased stability.

The dragon face kite at right is covered with lightweight, closely woven cloth on which the design is painted. To prevent stiffening of cloth from paint, use more solvent to thin it. The mouth is an opening lined with tape to prevent tearing. It can be closed with clear plastic.

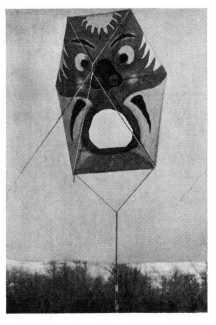

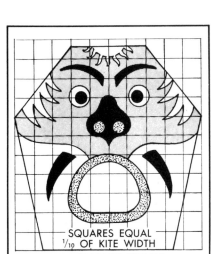

SQUARES EQUAL
1/10 OF KITE WIDTH

DRAGON-FACE DESIGN
ALL AREAS OUTLINED IN BLACK
SHADED AREAS — MEDIUM BLUE
DOTTED AREAS — RED
OTHER AREAS — WHITE OR BLACK
OPENING CUT INSIDE LIPS. CUT
EDGES ARE REINFORCED WITH TAPE

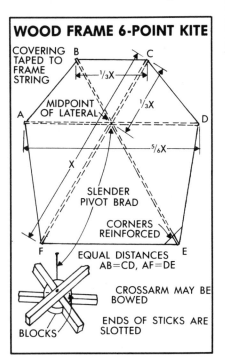

WOOD FRAME 6-POINT KITE

COVERING TAPED TO FRAME STRING

MIDPOINT OF LATERAL

1/3X

1/3X

5/6X

X

SLENDER PIVOT BRAD

CORNERS REINFORCED

EQUAL DISTANCES
AB=CD, AF=DE

CROSSARM MAY BE BOWED

ENDS OF STICKS ARE SLOTTED

BLOCKS

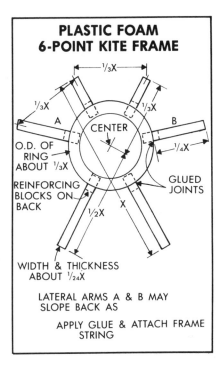

**PLASTIC FOAM
6-POINT KITE FRAME**

1/3X

1/3X

1/3X

CENTER

1/4X

O.D. OF RING ABOUT 1/3X

GLUED JOINTS

REINFORCING BLOCKS ON BACK

1/2X

X

WIDTH & THICKNESS ABOUT 1/24X

LATERAL ARMS A & B MAY SLOPE BACK AS

APPLY GLUE & ATTACH FRAME STRING

BRIDLES AND BALANCING

A 4-point kite not bowed needs a 4-string bridle (see below). If it is bowed a 2-string bridle AB is sufficient. A 6-point kite requires a 4-string bridle. Size of bridle string should be the same as that of the kite string — or just as strong. Tie the upper ends of the bridle to the sticks at equal distances from the tips and close to them, but attach the lower ends of the bridle farther from the lower tips to equalize strain on the sticks and minimize possibility of breakage. Tape reinforces the covering where the bridle passes through it. On plastic foam frames, the bridle is passed through the material with a darning needle. A short dowel under the tie on the back keeps the cord from cutting through.

Tie the bridle strings together to form a loop at the exact point where you find the kite in balance, so the side tips are equidistant from a level surface and the kite hangs at an angle of 20 to 30 degrees. The distance of the loop to the covering when the bridle is held taut should be about equal to one-third of the kite height.

The tail hitch is similarly fastened. Length of a tail hitch for a 4-point kite is not important. On a 6-point kite the distance from the loop to the kite should equal half the kite height. Also, the loop knot must be at the exact center of balance as shown in lower left detail.

Loops in the bridle and tail hitch facilitate attachment of the kite string and tail. A short dowel tied at the end of the kite string, lower center, is simply slipped through the bridle loop. A knot in the tail is brought through the loop of the tail hitch. Another way to attach a kite string to the bridle loop is by using a slip knot, lower right. To loosen this you simply pull the free end.

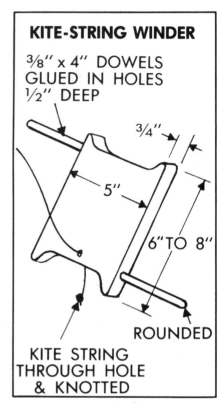

KITE-STRING WINDER

3/8" x 4" DOWELS GLUED IN HOLES 1/2" DEEP

3/4"

5"

6" TO 8"

ROUNDED

KITE STRING THROUGH HOLE & KNOTTED

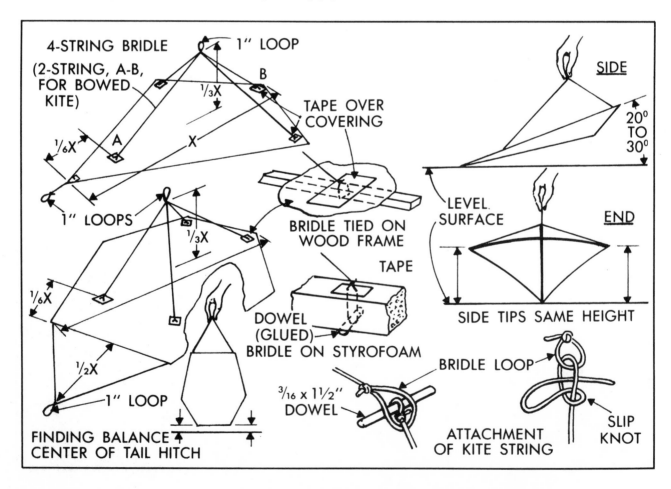

4-STRING BRIDLE (2-STRING, A-B, FOR BOWED KITE)

1" LOOP

B

1/3 X

A

1/6 X

X

TAPE OVER COVERING

1" LOOPS

1/3 X

BRIDLE TIED ON WOOD FRAME

TAPE

1/6 X

DOWEL (GLUED)
BRIDLE ON STYROFOAM

1/2 X

1" LOOP

FINDING BALANCE
CENTER OF TAIL HITCH

3/16 x 1 1/2" DOWEL

SIDE

20° TO 30°

LEVEL SURFACE

END

SIDE TIPS SAME HEIGHT

BRIDLE LOOP

ATTACHMENT OF KITE STRING

SLIP KNOT

WOOD FRAME SQUARE BOX KITE

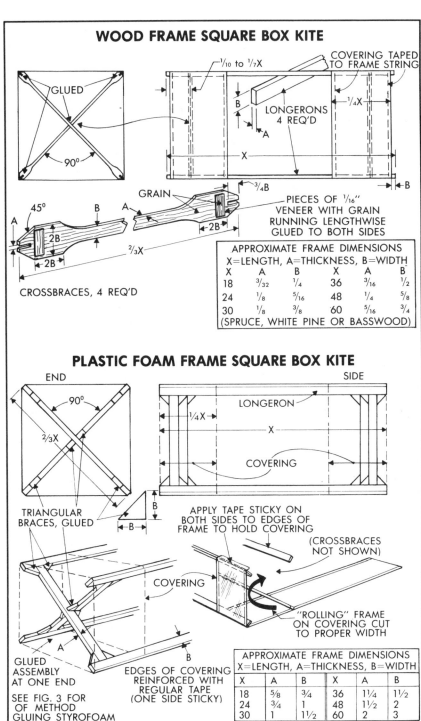

GLUED

90°

$^{1}/_{10}$ to $^{1}/_{7}$X

COVERING TAPED TO FRAME STRING

B

A

LONGERONS 4 REQ'D

$^{1}/_{4}$X

X

B

$^{3}/_{4}$B

45°

B

A

GRAIN

A

PIECES OF $^{1}/_{16}$" VENEER WITH GRAIN RUNNING LENGTHWISE GLUED TO BOTH SIDES

2B

2B

$^{2}/_{3}$X

2B

CROSSBRACES, 4 REQ'D

APPROXIMATE FRAME DIMENSIONS					
X=LENGTH, A=THICKNESS, B=WIDTH					
X	A	B	X	A	B
18	$^{3}/_{32}$	$^{1}/_{4}$	36	$^{3}/_{16}$	$^{1}/_{2}$
24	$^{1}/_{8}$	$^{5}/_{16}$	48	$^{1}/_{4}$	$^{5}/_{8}$
30	$^{1}/_{8}$	$^{3}/_{8}$	60	$^{5}/_{16}$	$^{3}/_{4}$
(SPRUCE, WHITE PINE OR BASSWOOD)					

PLASTIC FOAM FRAME SQUARE BOX KITE

END

SIDE

90°

$^{2}/_{3}$X

LONGERON

$^{1}/_{4}$X

X

COVERING

B

B

TRIANGULAR BRACES, GLUED

APPLY TAPE STICKY ON BOTH SIDES TO EDGES OF FRAME TO HOLD COVERING

(CROSSBRACES NOT SHOWN)

COVERING

A

B

"ROLLING" FRAME ON COVERING CUT TO PROPER WIDTH

GLUED ASSEMBLY AT ONE END

SEE FIG. 3 FOR OF METHOD GLUING STYROFOAM

EDGES OF COVERING REINFORCED WITH REGULAR TAPE (ONE SIDE STICKY)

APPROXIMATE FRAME DIMENSIONS					
X=LENGTH, A=THICKNESS, B=WIDTH					
X	A	B	X	A	B
18	$^{5}/_{8}$	$^{3}/_{4}$	36	$1^{1}/_{4}$	$1^{1}/_{2}$
24	$^{3}/_{4}$	1	48	$1^{1}/_{2}$	2
30	1	$1^{1}/_{2}$	60	2	3

Square box kites can be made with either wood or plastic foam frames. Slot the ends of wood cross braces and glue on small pieces of 1/16 in. veneer with its grain at right angles to that of the braces. The slots should fit snugly on the longerons. Glue the frame joints and adjust so the cross braces are equidistant from the ends of the longerons and at right angles to them. Cut the covering to required width and reinforce its side edges with tape. Then "roll" the frame onto the covering, lower right. No frame string is needed.

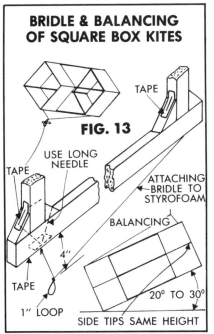

BRIDLE & BALANCING OF SQUARE BOX KITES

TAPE

USE LONG NEEDLE

TAPE

ATTACHING BRIDLE TO STYROFOAM

FIG. 13

BALANCING

4"

TAPE

1" LOOP

20° TO 30°

SIDE TIPS SAME HEIGHT

Cross braces of a plastic foam frame are closer to the ends of the longerons than they are in a wood frame. Follow the procedure of using polystyrene plastic cement as already explained. Tie the bridle string to a wood frame, but "stitch" it to a plastic foam frame with a darning needle after applying tape to prevent the cord from pulling through.

A simple parachute and release mechanism are shown here. A sail of light cardboard brings it to the kite. When the large loop strikes a trip stick at the end of the kite string, the wire holding the sail and parachute slips back to drop them, after which the gadget slides down to the starting point for repeat performance. Sixteen gauge steel wire is suitable.

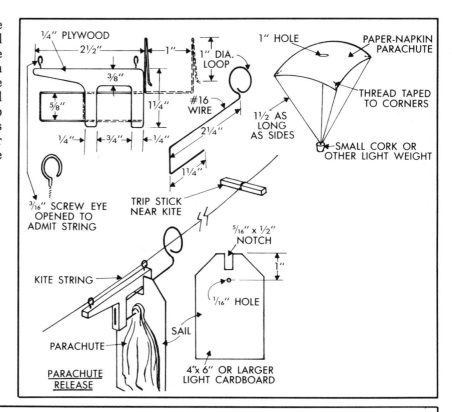

Table A   Characteristics of Various Woods For Use As Kite Sticks

Kind	Weight	Bending Strength	Stiffness	Kind	Weight	Bending Strength	Stiffness
Ash (white commercial)	41	110	161	Hickory (pignut)	53	144	198
Basswood	26	61	126	Maple (sugar)	44	114	178
Beech	45	102	169	Norway pine (red)	34	85	163
Birch (Alaska white)	38	89	161	Oak (red)	44	99	164
Cedar (red western)	23	60	108	Poplar (yellow)	28	71	135
Cottonwood (eastern)	28	62	123	Spruce (red)	28	72	138
Douglas fir (western)	34	90	181	Spruce (white)	28	68	123
Fir (balsam)	26	59	118	White pine (north)	25	63	119

Numerals given are comparative figures. Thickness and width of kite sticks as given with 4-point wood kite frame for spruce, white pine and basswood, can be reduced for heavier woods having greater bending strength and stiffness, to obtain comparable weight.

Table B   Size of Kite String or Twine

Kite Height	Material
12 to 24″	Store string
30″	#18, 36-lb. polished cotton twine or #6, 49-lb. nylon seine twine
36″	#24, 49-lb. polished cotton twine or #6, 49-lb. nylon seine twine
48″	#36, 73-lb. polished cotton twine or #9, 81-lb. nylon seine twine
60″	#48, 101-lb. polished cotton twine or #15, 114-lb. nylon seine twine
72″	#60, 123-lb. polished cotton twine or #18, 148-lb. nylon seine twine

(Numerals before lbs. indicate approximate breaking strength)

Table C   Type and Weight of Covering Materials

Kite Height	Material
12 to 24″	Japanese rice paper or polyethylene sheet plastic*
24 to 48″	No. 30 Kraft paper or polyethylene sheet plastic*
48 to 72″	No. 40 Kraft paper, lightweight, closely-woven cloth or polyethylene sheet plastic, 1½ mil.

*Grade used for wrapping food for freezers or thinner material used for dropcloths.

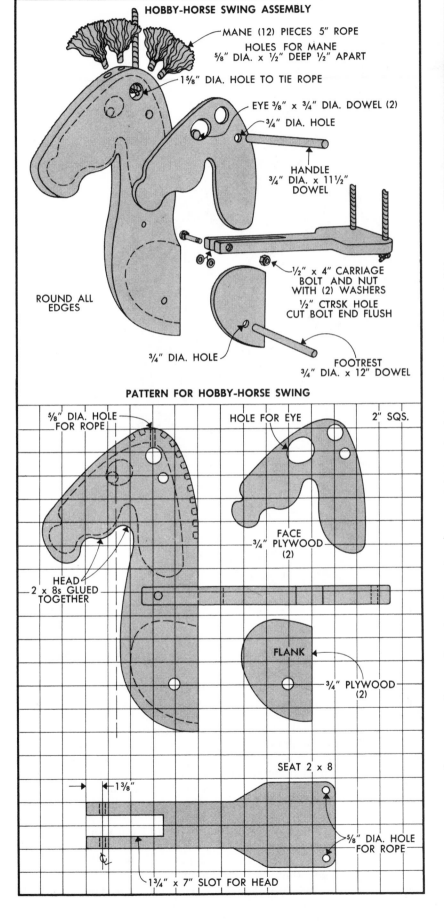

HOBBY-HORSE SWING ASSEMBLY

MANE (12) PIECES 5" ROPE

HOLES FOR MANE
5/8" DIA. x 1/2" DEEP 1/2" APART

1 5/8" DIA. HOLE TO TIE ROPE

EYE 3/8" x 3/4" DIA. DOWEL (2)

3/4" DIA. HOLE

HANDLE
3/4" DIA. x 11 1/2" DOWEL

ROUND ALL EDGES

1/2" x 4" CARRIAGE BOLT AND NUT WITH (2) WASHERS

1/2" CTRSK HOLE CUT BOLT END FLUSH

3/4" DIA. HOLE

FOOTREST
3/4" DIA. x 12" DOWEL

PATTERN FOR HOBBY-HORSE SWING

5/8" DIA. HOLE FOR ROPE

HOLE FOR EYE

2" SQS.

FACE
3/4" PLYWOOD (2)

HEAD
2 x 8s GLUED TOGETHER

FLANK

3/4" PLYWOOD (2)

SEAT 2 x 8

1 3/8"

5/8" DIA. HOLE FOR ROPE

1 3/4" x 7" SLOT FOR HEAD

Hobby-horse swing

A heavy favorite among the little folks is this easily built little swing. The main portion of the horse can be pieces of 2 x 8 edge glued together, or you can use two thicknesses of 3/4 in. marine plywood to create the required 1-1/2 in. stock.

Enlarge the squared drawings to make patterns from which the various parts are marked and cut.

The faces and flanks are cut out and glued to the main portion of the head after it is sawed to shape. Also bore the large hole that permits the knotted rope to firmly support the head. This hole is bored through both faces as well as the head.

Holes for the eyes are sawed and shaped in the faces before they are attached. The hole for the handle is drilled through both faces and the head after assembly.

A 1/2 in. carriage bolt is used as a pivot, with both the head and nut recessed. To assure long wear of the pivot, bore the holes 11/16 in. and drive in pieces of 1/2 in. thin-wall tubing to provide "bearing" surfaces for the pivot bolt.

Lengths of 1/2 in. rope are used to create the mane, and the swing also is suspended by three nylon ropes from a common point.

Note that 5/8 in. holes are specified for the 1/2 in. rope. This is because the rope actually is a bit larger than 1/2 in. and simply will not fit in a 1/2 in. diameter hole.

Wherever you decide to suspend the swing, be sure the suspension mount is anchored securely and will support at least twice the weight of the biggest child to ride it, just to be doubly safe.

Kiddie store

There are touches of magic, with perhaps a hint of Hansel and Gretel, in this charming little store that is right out of the land of make-believe. Set up indoors or out, the store can be stocked with make-believe groceries or with homemade cookies, candy, lemonade or other soft drinks for the hungry and thirsty to enjoy.

The store is a fun project that is easy to build. Two 4 x 8 ft. panels of 3/8 in. plywood are required, plus a few pieces of solid stock for the counter, windowsills and shelves.

It's best to leave the back open, so it can be placed against a wall. The full-width shelves at the back are "locked" into cleats with dowels to reinforce the structure, and the roof with its deep cleats holds the walls firmly in place.

The front of the store and each side wall are shaped and assembled separately. When complete, the three components are hinged together so they fold into a thin, compact "package" that can be stored easily. The two roof panels

also are hinged so they fold together. The 1 x 4 ridge boards provide added strength to the roof, and extra thickness for driving the screws that hold the hinges.

The 4 x 6 ft. front panel and one 2 x 4 ft. side wall are cut from one 4 x 8 ft. sheet of plywood, while the other side wall and both roof panels are cut from a second sheet. The scrap from window openings and each side of the triangular shape gable is used for the ornaments, shutters and trim.

The removable counter is made

from 1 in. stock, the ends notched to fit snugly around the window frame. A cleat is fastened in back to hold the counter in position and two hinged brackets are added to support the front portion of the counter.

The full-length shelves at the back (two or three, depending on your preference) are lengths of 1 x 4 with dowels glued near the ends in blind holes that fit in holes in cleats on the side walls.

Window openings in the side walls have windowsills 3 in. wide fastened permanently in place. The inside edge of the sill is flush with the inside of the wall to allow it to fold flat against the front. You can make one sill removable so the

other side wall folds flat against it.

Shutters on each side of the windows are merely ornamental. The design is cut with a jig or saber saw and the shutters are bradded and glued permanently to the side walls. The ornament on the peak of the roof is fitted with dowels in the lower edge. These dowels fit in holes bored in the ridge boards. The ornamental panels are glued and bradded in place as indicated.

When the carpentry work is complete, sand all parts, both inside and out, and apply a prime coat of paint. When the prime coat is dry, fill any nail holes, cracks or other defects with putty, sand smooth and apply the finish paint.

MATERIALS LIST

3/8″ plywood
Side, 24″ x 48″ (2)
Front, 48″ x 72″ (1)
Roof panel, 28″ x 48″ (2)
3/4″ plywood or 1″ solid stock
Roof cleat, 1″ x 1″ x 24″ (2), ripped diagonally to create 4 pieces
Shutter, 5-3/4″ x 16″ (4)
Side counter, 3″ x 18″ (2)
Front counter, 11″ x 43″ (1)
Squirrel cutout, 12″ x 18″ (1)
Ridge boards, 1 x 4 x 28″ (2)
Side decorator panel, 10″ x 18″ (2)
Front decorator panel, lower, 10″ x 43″ (1)
Front decorator panel, upper, 16″ x 27″ (1)
Front decorator panel, center, 8″ x 22″ (2)
Front counter bracket, 6″ x 8″ (2)
Shelves, 1 x 4 x 47-1/4″ (3)

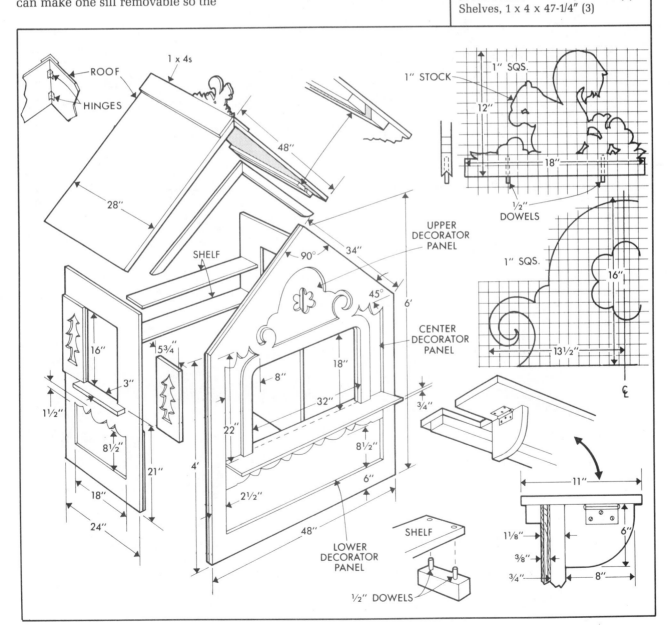

Using prefab construction permits taking preassembled frame sections to assembly site at road.

"Test run" before putting on siding showed that three children can sit comfortably on the seat.

School kids' bus-stop shelter

In the northlands where Arctic blasts of freezing weather occur all winter long, or farther south where wind and rain are the problem, this sturdy roadside shelter will protect two or three children from the elements. With its back to the prevailing winds and windows to watch through for the bus, it's high enough to accommodate most students from kindergarten right through high school, so build it to withstand years of weathering.

The building project is most easily done by prefabricating sections of the shelter in the workshop, then assembling it on site.

Cut all the framing lumber, mostly 2 x 2s, to length, and predrill for 10 penny galvanized box nails. Assemble the front, the back and the side frames as well as the seat and the base frames. Drill and countersink holes to permit screwing the various frames to the base and to each other.

For a permanent installation, pour a level concrete slab to support the shelter. Embedding bolts in the wet cement to bolt down the base is recommended for particularly windy areas.

Carry the frames to the building site, assemble and add 2 x 2 stretchers from front to back, with the top, ridge stretcher extended 2 in. past the front wall. Hold the angle frames in place and mark them, then cut to the marks. Attach plastic windows with duct tape, which allows the plywood or siding to seal them. The assembled framing and the roof are most easily covered with exterior or preferably marine plywood.

If plywood is used for the roof only, use cutting diagram B, with the base plywood in two pieces. Use diagram A if all plywood is used; the roofs and seat will be cut from a second sheet, with some left for another job.

Windows can be cut from rigid plastic, held to framing with duct tape that is water and weather resistant.

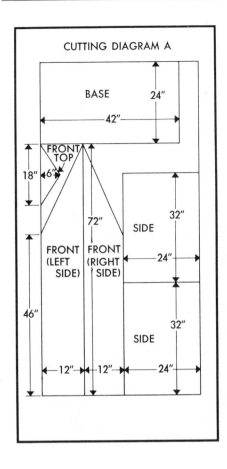

CUTTING DIAGRAM A

BASE 24"
42"

FRONT TOP
18" 6"
FRONT (LEFT SIDE) FRONT (RIGHT SIDE)
72"
46"
12" 12" 24"

SIDE 32"
24"
SIDE 32"

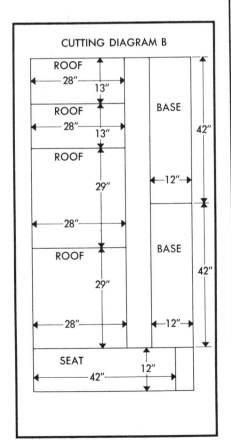

CUTTING DIAGRAM B

ROOF
28"
13"
ROOF
28"
13"
ROOF
29"
28"
ROOF
29"
28"
SEAT
42" 12"

BASE
42"

BASE
42"

12"

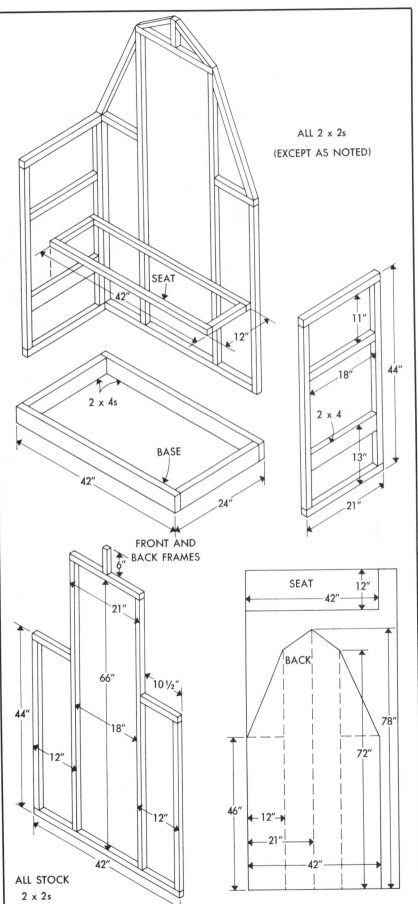

ALL 2 x 2s
(EXCEPT AS NOTED)

SEAT
42"
12"

2 x 4s
BASE
42"
24"

FRONT AND
BACK FRAMES

11"
18"
44"
2 x 4
13"
21"

ALL STOCK
2 x 2s

6"
21"
44"
66"
18"
10½"
12"
12"
42"

SEAT
42" 12"
BACK
78"
72"
46" 12"
21"
42"

Convertible playhouse/toolshed

Any little girl or boy would be delighted to have a playhouse, and Dad will appreciate it too when it's designed for later use as a storage shed for lawnmowers and other yard and garden tools after the kids have outgrown it.

The back panel is held with Tee-Nuts, which permits it to be removed and replaced with a fair-sized door that will allow rolling in a garden tractor or a power lawnmower. If it is to be used for winter storage when it's too cold for the children to use, then the back panel can be hinged and fitted with a latch.

Start construction by making a platform frame of 2 x 4s that is 72 in. each way. The full-length joists are spiked to the end members of the platform; the shorter cross-pieces are staggered in alternate spaces so spikes can be driven through the longer joists into the ends of the shorter 2 x 4s. Exterior grade 3/4 in. plywood is nailed to the framework next.

The finished floor assembly is now set up on four or more concrete blocks to keep the playhouse off the ground. Level it up in both directions to permit easy plumbing of the walls. The top and bottom plates of the walls, as well as the interior studs, are 1 x 2s, while the end studs are 2 x 2s. Make the side walls first; they are the full 72 in. long and 43-5/8 in. high. Spike them to the floor and temporarily brace them plumb. The plywood siding isn't applied until the frames of all four walls are spiked to the floor.

The front wall is next. Note that the top plate goes all the way across, but the bottom plate is cut out for the door. You can later add a door sill, if you wish. The back wall is framed as indicated, with the top and bottom plates full length. The removable panel is made to fit inside the center section of the wall framing, a clearance of 1/8 in. being allowed at top and bottom. The overall length of the front and back wall framing is shorter by twice the width of the inside walls, as indicated. The plywood siding is now nailed to the side walls, and extended down over the floor framing. It will run from the top of the side walls down, if the 4 ft. width of a 4 x 8 ft.

sheet is used, but will have to be spliced for the front and back walls. Triangular shapes will have to be cut to fit the eaves above the front and back walls. Battens, cut from lengths of trellis wood, are nailed over all joints and spaced along the side walls over the wall studs to make a more uniform pattern.

The roof will require three sheets of 1/2 in. exterior plywood. Two full sheets are nailed to the rafters at the lower edge, then the third sheet is ripped down the center lengthwise and each half is nailed on the roof to meet at the ridge. Building felt next is nailed to the roof. Over this is tacked household aluminum foil to act as reflective insulation. The final covering of the roof is shingles. Five bundles of second course shingles are required.

The door and the shutters for the playhouse now are made. While dimensions are given for these, we suggest you measure the openings in the structure you build, and size them accordingly. Allow 1/8 in. clearance in both width and length to make sure shutters and door open and close easily.

Paint the house with at least two coats of house paint, perhaps to match your home. It would be a good idea to prime the backs of all the battens before nailing them in place, and caulk around all joints, as you would in a real home. Glass is not recommended for the windows when it is used as a playhouse because of the hazard to small children, but screens or clear sheet plastic in the windows and door would be a fine idea.

Basic structure before front window is cut out, door not installed.

Finished back panel with battens over joints, shutters installed over window.

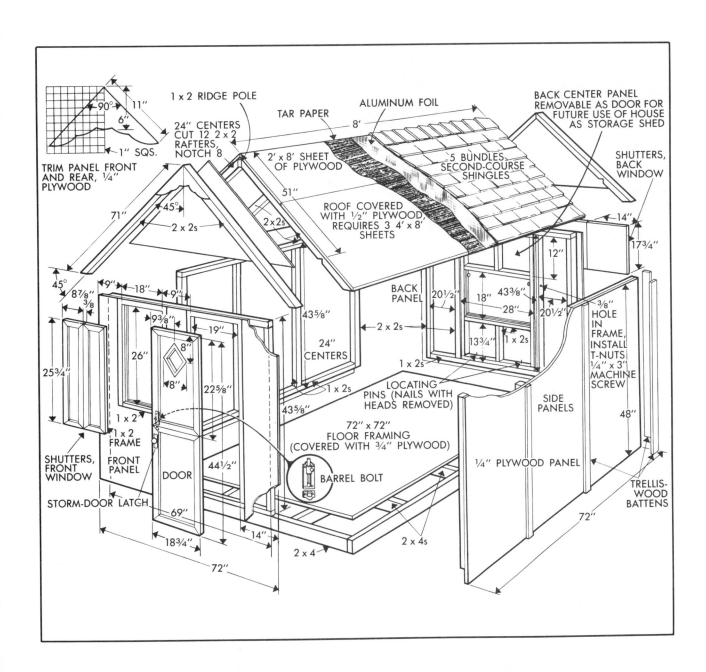

Scandinavian playhouse

Shielding its occupants from rain or snow or baking sun, this half porch Scandinavian playhouse will make your children the envy of all their playmates.

Particleboard, exterior grade, is suggested for the floor, walls and roof because of its low cost, but exterior grade plywood could be substituted if particleboard is not available. Where high winds might be a problem, the nailing strips could be increased in size to 2 x 4s to provide additional strength. We also suggest "back-priming" all members. That is painting the back sides and edges that will be hidden in the final assembly. This will assure better weatherproofing and longer life for the structure.

Clear sheet plastic could be installed in the window to provide light and keep out wind and rain. You may want to buy a couple of bundles of shingles to match those on the roof of your house in order to assure a more weathertight roof.

Start construction of the playhouse by spiking together 2 x 4s to create the "foundation." Use 16 penny galvanized box nails.

If you build the structure outside, set the foundation on bricks or concrete blocks to keep it off the ground. If you build it inside for assembly outside when the weather is warm, simply nail the floor to the foundation frame.

Side walls are next, made by cutting a 4 x 4 ft. sheet of plywood or particleboard in half. Attach the nailing strips and prop the walls on them, then set the walls on the foundation. Make the back wall and nail it to the nailing strips on the side walls.

If the house is to be assembled outside later, just tack nail the assembly. If you will be taking the house apart each fall and storing it away, then use nuts and bolts.

The front wall is the same shape as the back wall, but has the door opening cut in it which is framed with 1 x 4s. For the more creative, the trim could be scalloped or carved to more closely simulate the Viking heritage of the structure.

The posts that support the free end of the roof over the porch are assembled from 1 x 4s to a T-shape as indicated. The roof truss is fabricated as shown, then fitted to the posts. A short length of 1 x 4 is nailed to the posts and the truss to reinforce the joint.

The railing is assembled from pieces cut to the sizes and shapes shown, then fitted between the house wall and the posts. The roof halves are next, each being a full 4 x 8 ft. sheet of material. Then the two benches are assembled and fitted in place between the front wall and posts. The door is a sheet of plywood or particleboard with battens nailed to it vertically, horizontally or in a pattern, to suit your own taste. Initials or an address might be a fanciful decoration.

All pieces should have been back-primed as suggested earlier, and the completed structure now should be given two coats of house paint. Paint the trim a contrasting color.

A very practical modification for the playhouse would be to hinge the back wall so you could use the structure for winter storage of a lawnmower and other yard and garden equipment and tools. Hinges could be fitted to one vertical edge of the back wall, or at the bottom. In the latter case, the wall then could be a ramp up which a lawnmower or a lightweight garden tractor could be rolled.

It wouldn't be too difficult to install plastic windows in the side walls for even more light.

"Foundation" is 2 x 4s with floor of exterior grade particleboard.

Use nails for permanent structure, bolts for "take-apart."

Full 4 x 8 ft. sheet of material is used for each side of roof.

Nailing strips on edges allow attaching to each other with nails or bolts.

"Truss" for porch roof, columns and railings are next. Keep columns plumb.

Final steps are installation of benches, trimming to fit, hanging of door, painting.

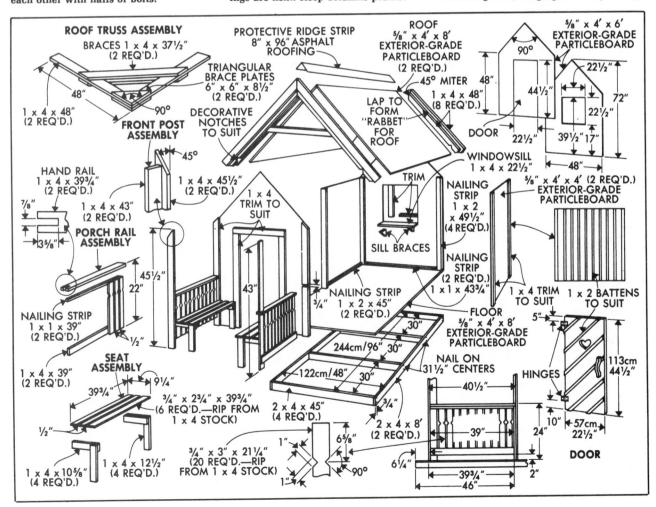

Storybook playhouse/slide

This storybook playhouse was inspired by the nursery rhyme about the old woman who lived in a shoe.

Double check your measurements before cutting. The dimensions given are the dimensions of the actual stock used in building the original, but these will vary with differences in stock size.

To begin construction, lay three sheets of 1/8 in. tempered hardboard on a flat surface with smooth side up. Make sure all edges are butted tight and lay out a grid of 6 in. squares on the surface as shown in drawing. Once you have marked the sheets for parts A-1, B-1 and C-1, saw the pieces and use these as patterns for parts A-2, B-2 and C-2.

To make the back, another sheet of 1/8 in. hardboard is marked and cut. Cut the 1 x 3 frame pieces for the back so the ends of each piece stop 3/4 in. from the edge of the hardboard. Glue and brad the pieces into position.

Before starting assembly of the sides, decide on which side of the shoe you want the door. Refer to the squared drawing for dimensions and cut the opening in the appropriate piece — either A-1 or A-2. Use the cutout as the door. Place pieces A-1, B-1 and C-1 smooth side up on a flat surface and align all edges. Cut one end of a 1 x 3 x 10 ft. to 83-1/2 degrees and notch the other end to accept a 1 x 3. This is shown in the drawing as Part 1. Apply waterproof glue to the frame member and slip it under the side pieces, positioning it so it meets point Z and is flush with the bottom edge. Then drive brads through the hardboard and into the member.

Now, turn the assembly over and attach frame members 2, 3, 4 and 5 using the reference points V, W, X and Y. Join these pieces with corrugated fasteners but do not glue or brad them to the sides at this time. If this is the side which the door will be on, then add parts 9 and 10 too. Next, notch pieces 6, 7 and 8 to accept the 1 x 3 cross

members and add them. Now that the frame is complete apply glue to the surface of the frame and brad the side pieces to it. Make the second frame for the opposite side of the shoe.

Next, make the cross members that support the slide by cutting eleven 1 x 3s and one 1 x 4 to 24 in. Make an 83-1/2 degree angle on one edge of a 1 x 3 and use this piece at the top where the back wall and platform meet. Cut a 45 degree angle on one edge of the 1 x 3 that joins the slide and platform. Assemble the shoe by placing one side down and gluing and bradding the back into position. Stand this assembly upright and glue and brad the second side into position. Attach a cross member into the notch at the end of Part 1 and attach the 1 x 15 x 24 in. piece of hardboard in the toe. This piece is cut from a full sheet of 1/4 in. hardboard; the remainder is for the slide and platform.

Install the cross members using glue and nailing through the sides and into the ends of each member. Rip the remainder of the 1/4 in. hardboard to create two pieces 24 in. wide. Make the upper section of the slide by cutting 36 in. from the shorter piece and making a 45 degree angle at each end, as shown. When installing, make sure the piece is flush with Part 6. Next, cut the platform to fit, and glue and brad it into place. Now, cut the remaining piece of hardboard to 84 in. and make a 45 degree angle at

one end so it neatly joins the hardboard used at the upper end of the slide. Apply glue to the supports, then tap the piece into position, securing with brads at the edges.

Now add the 1 x 4 side rails, a, b, c and the fillet, by gluing and nailing through the sides. Sand round and smooth the joints of the rails and all other sharp joints or edges.

Attach the ladder with glue and screws, driving the screws into the rails from inside the shoe. The top of the shoe is trimmed with a pair of 1-1/4 x 30 in. dowels dadoed 1/8 x 3/8 in. deep. Glue the rails into position. Finally, make a simple frame for the door out of 1 x 3s and attach the hardboard with glue and brads. Hang the door with butt hinges.

MATERIALS LIST

a, 1 x 4 x 22-1/2" (2)
b, 1 x 4 x 87-1/2" (2)
c, 1 x 4 x 34" (2)
d, 1-1/4" x 30" dowels (2)
e, 1-1/4" x 24" dowels (9)
f, 1 x 4, cut to fit (2)
1, 1 x 3 x 95-3/4" (2)
2, 1 x 3 x 74" (2)
3, 1 x 3 x 55" (2)
4, 1 x 3 x 7" (2)
5, 1 x 3 x 7" (2)
6, 1 x 3 x 16" (2)
7, 1 x 3 x 95" (2)
8, 1 x 3 x 30" (2)
9, 1 x 4 x 42-1/2"
10, 1 x 3, cut to fit
11, 1 x 3 x 40-1/2"
12, 1 x 3 x 73-1/4"
13, 1 x 3 x 73-1/4"

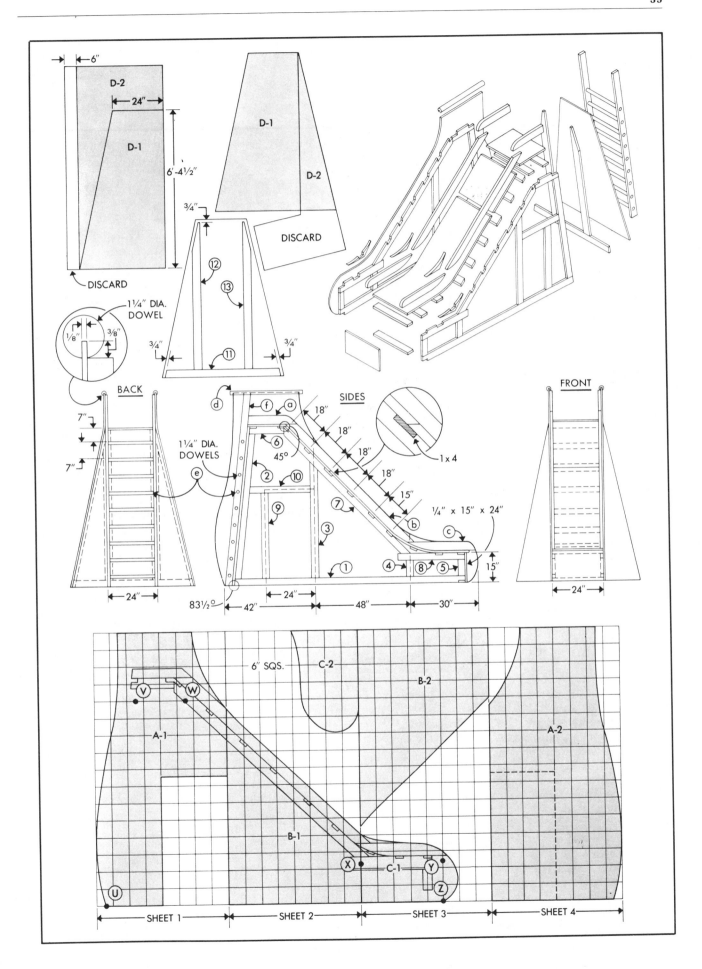

Two-story playhouse/storeroom

Tree houses are fun and playhouses are great, but this design combines the best of both. It also provides Mom and Dad with a secure place to store all those garden tools, lawnmower, bicycles and other odds and ends that usually are crammed into the family garage.

The ground level storage room has a full 6 ft. of headroom, so most adults can stand without stooping. The upper level combines a weathertight playhouse with an outdoor deck protected by a short wall rather than an open railing.

The foundation is the first step, a concrete slab. Check local building codes for specifications on the slab; it usually is necessary to dig a trench around the perimeter of the slab to provide a footing. The foundation shown was raised above the ground the width of a 2 x 4 to keep the siding free of mud splash.

The 2 x 4s used for forms were salvaged, cleaned of concrete and used for blocking and spacers in the framing. Anchor bolts were placed in the concrete before it set and spaced so they were located between the wall studs.

The first wall framed is one of the shorter 6 ft. end ones. Assemble the plates and studs on a flat surface. Make sure the framing is square before spiking in the angled bracing.

Bore the anchor bolt holes in the bottom plate a bit oversize so the framing can be moved slightly if necessary to align corners. Use flat washers under the nuts of the anchor bolts to provide a full bearing surface for the nuts.

Build the frame for the front wall next, using block-spaced double studs for outside corners. Cut the corner studs for the second story playhouse to a length of 11 ft. 1 in., but leave the rest of the 6 ft. and 12 ft. 2 x 4 studs full length to be marked and cut later. Note that 2 x 4 spacer blocks for the upper floor are top nailed into support blocks spiked to the studs. Do not bolt the

front wall to the slab.

The three gussets for the roof trusses are layed out on 3 ft. lengths of 1 x 6 and cut to shape. Cut the ten roof rafters and make bird's mouth notches in the six that will be used for trusses. Plumb and brace the front wall, then place one of the trusses across the framing and mark the upper ends of the studs for final trimming. Take down the framing and place it on a flat surface while you cut the studs to the proper length and angle.

Bolt the framing to the slab and spike it to the adjacent wall framing. When the remaining two walls

have been framed and set, the two outside 2 x 6 joists for the upper floor can be cut and nailed in place. Cut and fit the outside 2 x 6 block, then lay up the two inside joists and nail the end header joist in place.

Cut the 1/2 in. plywood floor sections to size, make the cutout for the trap door, then nail down the floor. Cut the two 2 x 4 fascia pieces for the roof and nail them to the three trusses. After fitting and nailing the end rafters to the framing, fit the roof assembly in place and spike it securely. Note that the end rafters are cut to allow fitting the inside rafters for the roof extensions at the front and back of the playhouse.

Framing for the two second floor end walls should be completed next. The number, size and location of windows is optional.

When this playhouse was built, the framing for the roof extensions was fitted before the siding was added. Because of the extensive cutting and fitting of the siding around this framing, it is recommended that the siding be completed before framing for the roof extension is applied.

The corner posts for the wall around the deck are bolted to the ends of the 2 x 6 joist. Be sure to countersink the heads of the carriage bolts so the siding will lie flat when nailed to the framing of the short wall around the upper deck.

Cut and assemble the pieces for the three roof lookouts. Be sure they are positioned so the plywood roof decking they support will be flush with the decking on the front and back roof extension.

Siding is applied from the bottom up. The lower edge of the first strip is shimmed out from the framing by a piece of 3/8 in. stock 1-1/2 in. high. The strips of siding then are nailed to the wall framing with 2-1/2 in. galvanized box nails.

The top strips of siding are cut at an angle to match the roof. The notch in the rafter shown in one photo should be ignored; the fellow notching the rafters for the trusses notched it in error.

Lay out and cut the scrolled trim for the eaves on 1 x 6 stock. Fit and nail it in place with casing nails or finishing nails.

Apply the roof decking, then flash the ridges and valleys with 12 in. wide sheet aluminum.

The first step in roofing is a layer of roofing felt underlayment. The felt is applied from the eaves up, and held only with staples as the roofing is nailed over it.

The next step is to nail on a length of 36 in. wide mineral surfaced roofing to each edge of the roof. Tabs are cut off enough shingles to create a starter course for each eave that projects 1/4 in. along the eave and at each end and they are nailed over roofing strip.

Every other succeeding course is started with a shingle from which 6 in. has been cut. This assures that tabs and slots align to create a weathertight roof. The small size of the roof and the ease of aligning the shingles eliminates the need for the usual snapped chalk lines used to keep long courses straight and parallel.

Shingles on one roof surface are lapped 6 in. over the ridge and nailed down. The cap for the roofing is made by cutting 12 x 12 in. squares from the roll roofing and lapping 6 in. on each side of the roof. If the weather is cool, warm the squares with a hair dryer so they bend easily and do not crack.

Windowsills and jambs are cut from 1 x 8 stock and nailed with the outer edges flush with the siding. Trim then can be nailed to the casing and siding and all joints caulked. Windows are made of a simple box frame cut from 1-1/4 in. stair material. Because the structure is a playhouse, glaze with sheet plastic rather than glass.

Windows that open are hinged from the top to open outward. Dowels attached with screweyes are used to hold the windows open.

The two double crossbuck doors are made from 1/2 in. exterior grade plywood framed with 1-1/2 in. stair stock. The crossbuck trim is 3/4 in. stock nailed to the outside face of each door.

Details show how the round window is created and this will be a challenge no matter which of the methods shown is used.

The ladder leading up through the trap door is hung on screweyes driven into the joist under the upper deck. A rope allows youngsters on the deck to pull the ladder up so other children cannot climb up. For safety, Dad should have some kind of a snap hook to hold the ladder up when the family is away, to assure that neighborhood tots would not try to climb the ladder.

An alternate method would be to make the ladder removable so it could be stored in the house or basement, thus removing the temptation for children to try to enter the playhouse when the family is absent.

Pouring concrete slab foundation is first step. Form boards are salvaged and cleaned, then used in framing.

Short end walls are framed first, including diagonal braces. Make sure framing is level.

Wall frames are fitted over bolts in foundation, after holes are drilled in sill plate. Temporary braces hold framing vertical.

42

Higher side walls require at least two people to lift them into position. Shorter side wall will brace higher framing.

Roof framing, including gussets across rafters, is built on the ground, then lifted into place on wall framing.

Rafters are notched with "bird's mouths" to fit over top plates of walls. End rafter should not have been notched.

Posts for railing on upper deck are bolted to framing, rather than being nailed. This is needed safety factor.

Cut opening for trap door, then nail plywood flooring in place. Joints in plywood should be supported underneath.

Siding is nailed directly to framing, with nails at top and bottom of each strip.

Siding must be cut to match angle of roof in the top courses.

Doors are cut from panels of 1/2 in. exterior grade plywood; crossbucks and trim are cut from 3/4 in. material. Ladder is hung on screweyes. Rope goes to upper level.

Asphalt shingles are used on playhouse roof. They look good and are easily applied.

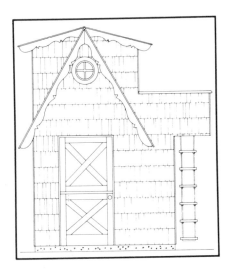

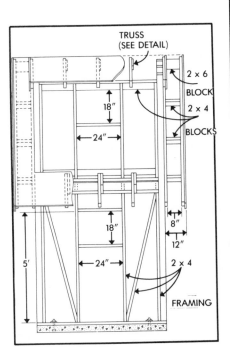

FRAMING

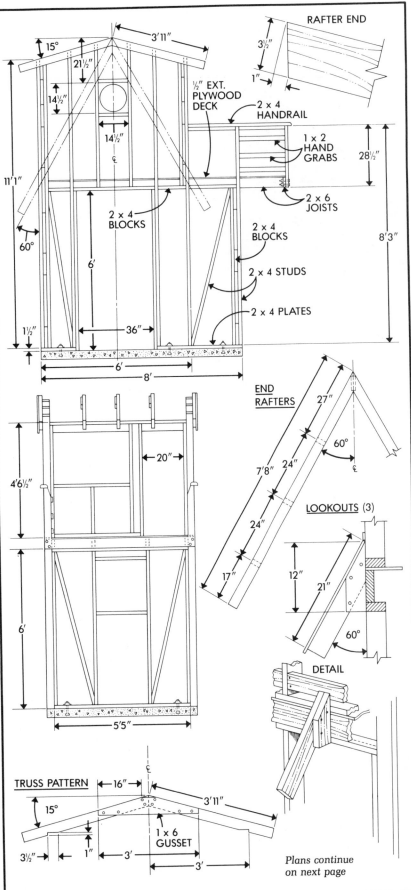

RAFTER END

3½"

1"

15°

3'11"

21½"

14½"

½" EXT. PLYWOOD DECK

2 x 4 HANDRAIL

1 x 2 HAND GRABS

28½"

14½"

11'1"

2 x 4 BLOCKS

2 x 6 JOISTS

2 x 4 BLOCKS

2 x 4 STUDS

8'3"

60°

6'

2 x 4 PLATES

1½"

36"

6'

8'

END RAFTERS

27"

60°

7'8"

24"

24"

17"

LOOKOUTS (3)

12"

21"

60°

4'6½"

20"

6'

DETAIL

5'5"

TRUSS PATTERN

16"

3'11"

15°

1 x 6 GUSSET

3½"

1"

3'

3'

Plans continue on next page

Youngsters on upper deck can swing up ladder by pulling on rope. A latch to hold ladder would be safety measure.

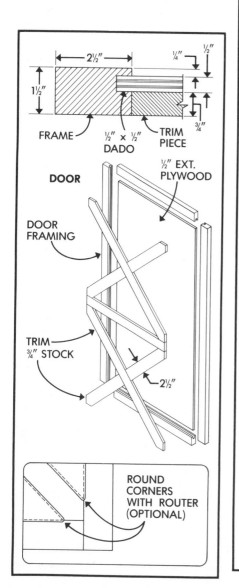

STORAGE AREA

STEEP ROOF LINE

6'
16" 16" 16"
6'
2' WINDOW
3' DOOR
3' 3'
8'

PLAYHOUSE

SECOND FLOOR

2 x 4 HANDRAIL
½" EXT. PLYWOOD DECK
2 x 6 BLOCK UNDER PLYWOOD JOINT
20" DOOR
2' WINDOW
2 x 6 BLOCK UNDER PLYWOOD JOINT
3' WINDOW
DRAIN SLOT
16"
17"
ROUND WINDOW 14½"
TRAP DOOR FRAMING
10'

DOOR

FRAME
½" × ½" DADO
TRIM PIECE
2½"
1½"
¼"
½"
¾"

DOOR FRAMING
½" EXT. PLYWOOD
TRIM ¾" STOCK
2½"

ROUND CORNERS WITH ROUTER (OPTIONAL)

ROUND WINDOW

18" OUTSIDE DIA.
2 x 4 STUD
14½"
13" INSIDE DIA.
ACRYLIC SHEET ⅛" × 14¼" × 14¼"
A
A
INSIDE FRAME ½" × 14½" × 14½"
OUTSIDE FRAME ½" × 18" DIA.
SPACER RING ¾" × 16½" DIA.
ACRYLIC SHEET

ALTERNATE INSIDE FRAME

4" ½"
CUT OUT SECTIONS
½"
14½"
13" DIA.
14½"

SECTION A—A

INSIDE FRAME
2 x 4 STUD
SIDING
ACRYLIC SHEET
SPACER
OUTSIDE FRAME

A-frame playhouse/storehouse

Extremely strong because of its shape, and weather resistant because it is all roof, this playhouse will provide years of fun for youngsters, and is a fine place to store lawn and garden tools in the winter or after the children have grown.

The A-frames are 12 ft. lengths of 2 x 4 joined at the top with an exterior grade plywood gusset. They are joined at the center with a 2 x 4 for the second floor and at the bottom are spaced 9 ft. apart. Build the three frames flat, then lift them into position on the floor that consists of two 4 x 4s boxed at the ends with 2 x 4s. Floor joists are 2 x 4s, between which short lengths of 2 x 4 are staggered and spiked for added rigidity.

In warm climates just tack up tar paper and cover it with siding; in colder climates you might want exterior plywood sheathing, plus shingles. The door and shutters can be made by nailing cleats to the siding, then cutting the section free and hinging it in place. Complete the door before finishing the roof, so you can get inside to cut out the windows.

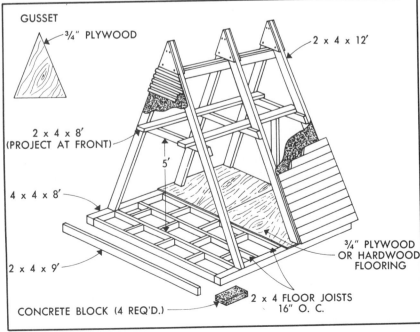

GUSSET

¾" PLYWOOD

2 x 4 x 12'

2 x 4 x 8'
(PROJECT AT FRONT)

5'

4 x 4 x 8'

¾" PLYWOOD
OR HARDWOOD
FLOORING

2 x 4 x 9'

2 x 4 FLOOR JOISTS
16" O. C.

CONCRETE BLOCK (4 REQ'D.)

Two-man bobsled

With its quick action, auto type steering and its light weight, this bobsled will be in a class by itself as it goes skimming down the slopes. The unique, skeletonized riding platform is light, yet strong and rigid.

Begin construction of the sled with the riding platform. Assemble it from strips, A-1 and A-2, and spacers A-3 with waterproof glue and screws. Cut the body cross members, B-1 and B-2, and drill 1-3/8 in. diameter holes in the ends as shown, Fig. 1. Fasten the cross members to the runner supports, C-1 and C-2, then fasten both runner assemblies to the body platform with bolts, washers and nuts. Note that front assembly is 1/4 in. wider than the platform to accommodate the hood side panels. At this point, you may wish to give the platform several coats of clear marine varnish, as parts of it will be hard to get to later.

Attach the four die cast shaft bearings to the back assembly as shown in Fig. 7.

Make the runners, G and H, from a good quality, springy stock such as ash, making sure it is straight grained and clear. After the runners are rough cut to shape, lay out the front and back radii, and saw them to shape as shown in Fig. 8. Cut a shallow groove in the bottom of each runner and sand smooth to final shape. Apply several coats of marine varnish, sanding between coats, and when glass hard, rub on several coats of beeswax. Make the runner mounts, E, and attach to each back runner, Fig. 10. The back runner mounts also have a bearing for the axle as shown. Cut and shape the tie rod, F, and the front runner mounts and extensions, D-1 and D-2, and fasten together as shown in Fig. 9. A 2 in. bolt will have to be passed up through them before they are attached to the runners. Position the two bolts in the center of the tie rod, that locates the steering rod, and position the tie rod and mounts together in their pivots with bolts, washers and nuts.

To make the "cowling" or front hood, enlarge the squared drawings of L and M, make patterns, and saw the curved frames from 1/2 in. stock. You will need four small and two large frames. Attach

a 5 in. spacer at the center shown in Fig. 3, and glue and screw the large frame pieces to the spacer. Fasten the vertical supports, N, to the platform and to the top ends of the frames. These joints are reinforced with plywood gussets, P. Cut the two inside panels, X, and fasten in place with glue and screws. Attach the two smaller hood frames, M, next to the hood panels, Fig. 4. Add spacers and attach the last two outside frames. These frames are also positioned with vertical supports and gussets.

At this point, construct and install the steering mechanism. If you don't have access to a welder, you will have to have someone else assemble this portion. Make sure before welding on the steering wheel flange plate and the column extension that you have one of the die cast bearings on the column.

The exact position of the upper and lower steering column brackets, J and K, will be determined by the height you intend to have the steering wheel. After you have worked this out, cut out the brackets and secure in place with bolts and screws. Position the steering column and fasten all collars, Fig. 4. Fig. 2 shows the lower steering mechanism from the underside.

With the steering column assembly in place and secured, attach the 1/8 in. plywood covering, R, to the center hood frame, using glue, screws and finishing washers. Cut the side hood coverings, Q, apply glue and fasten in place, clamping with blocks of wood as shown in Fig. 5. Smooth off all sharp edges and attach the outer side panels, Y, with glue and small screws. The outer side panels extend down to the lower edges of the platform members.

Glue up the laminated steering wheel as shown, rough cut to shape, Fig. 11, and finish with rasp and sandpaper. Attach the completed wheel to the flange, using 1/4 in. carriage bolts. Fit the closet pole footrests, S, on the underside of the platform and fasten with screws. Slide the hand grips, T,

through the holes in the cross members and fasten with glue and screws.

Paint the steering wheel and footrests black. For an especially sporty look, paint the hood and hand grips in bright colors.

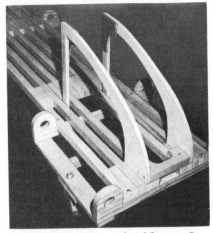

Fig. 3. Spacer positions hood frames. Supports and frames are held with gussets. Note bolts for cross members.

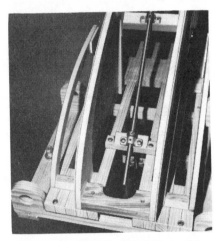

Fig. 4. Steering wheel height is determined, assembly is welded, fastened in place with brackets and collars.

Fig. 1. Riding platform is "grid" of hardwood strips and spacers. Holes in cross members are for hand grips.

Fig. 2. Underneath view of steering mechanism shows position of column extension in bolts on tie rod.

Fig. 5. Center hood covering is attached with glue, screws and finishing washers. Sides are glued, then clamped.

MATERIALS LIST

A-1, Longitudinals, ash, 1-1/8" x 1-1/8" x 6'6" (6)
A-2, Longitudinal, ash, 1-1/8" x 1-1/8" x 56" (1)
A-3, Spacers, ash, 1-1/8" x 1-1/8" x 5" (22)
B-1, Cross members, ash, 1" x 4-1/2" x 21-3/4" (2)
B-2, Cross members, ash, 1" x 4-1/2" x 22" (2)
C-1, Back runner support, ash, 3/4" x 3-1/2" x 23" (2)
C-2, Front runner support, ash, 3/4" x 2-1/2" x 18" (2)
D-1, Front runner mount, ash, 1-1/8" x 3" x 5" (2)
D-2, Mount extension, maple, 1/2" x 1-1/8" x 6" (2)
E, Back runner mount, ash, 1-1/4" x 3-1/4" x 8" (2)
F, Tie rod, ash, 1" x 3" x 21" (1)
G, Front runner, ash, 1-1/2" x 3-1/2" x 36" (1)
H, Back runner, ash, 1-1/2" x 3-1/2" x 36" (1)
I-1, Steering wheel, ash, 1/4" x 2-1/4" x 7" (4)
I-2, Steering wheel, ash, 1" x 3-3/4" x 12" (1)
I-3, Steering wheel, 1/2" x 1-5/8" x 2-1/4" (4)
J, Upper steering column bracket, ash, 1-1/4" x 1-1/2" x 6-3/8" (1)
K, Lower steering column bracket, ash, 1-1/4" x 1-1/2" x 5-5/8" (1)
L, Hood frame, ash, 1/2" x 8" x 26" (2)
M, Hood frame, ash, 1/2" x 4" x 22" (4)
N, Frame support, ash, 1/2" x 1-1/4" x 12-7/8" (2)
O, Frame support, ash, 1/2" x 1-1/4" x 6" (2)
P, Hood frame gusset, plywood, 1/4" x 2-1/2" x 4" (6)
Q, Lower hood covering, plywood, 1/8" x 3-3/8" x 23" (2)
R, Upper hood covering, plywood, 1/8" x 7-7/8" x 28" (1)
S, Footrests, fir dowel, 1-5/16" diameter x 36" (2)
T, Hand grips, fir dowel, 1-5/16" diameter x 6'6" (2)
U, Steering column, C.R.S., 1/2" diameter x 23" (1)
V, Steering wheel flange, steel plate, 1/4" x 3" diameter (1)
W, Column ext., C.R.S., 1/2" diameter x 9" (1)
X, Inside hood side panels, hardboard, 1/8" x 13" x 22" (2)
Y, Outside hood side panels, hardboard, 1/8" x 8" x 20" (2)

Fig. 6. Outside hood panels are extended to lower edge of platform, between platform and crosspieces.

Fig. 7. Four die cast bearings are fastened on runner mount assemblies to accept back axle and runners.

Fig. 8. Runners are rough cut from clear, straight grained stock such as ash, shaped with rasp and sandpaper.

Fig. 9. Tie rod and runner mount assembly is bolted to front runners after inserting bolts in mounts.

Fig. 10. Finish as you go. Platform and runners are finished natural, mounts black. Note bearings on mounts.

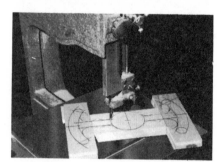

Fig. 11. Steering wheel is laminated from hardwood, rough sawn to shape, then finished with rasp and sandpaper.

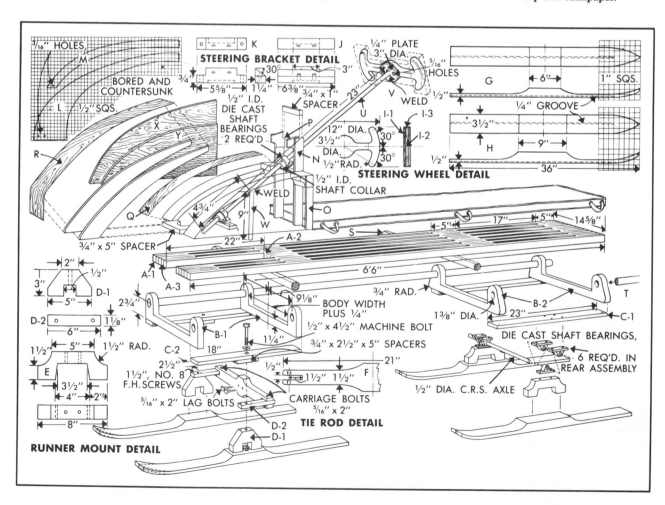

Russian toddler's sleigh

Patterned after a Russian sleigh, this scaled-down model for toddlers has an inner and outer shell cut from exterior grade plywood. Start by enlarging the squared drawings to make patterns for the two inner sides that are cut from one piece of plywood to economize on material, and the outer sides that are somewhat bigger. Make sure the curve at the front of the outer sides is smooth and even, and that both sides are identical.

If there is a "good" side to the plywood, make sure it is on the outside of the sides of the outer shell.

Cut the several pieces for the inner shell, the supports, braces, bottom, back, etc., and join the sides with the pieces, using waterproof glue and nails. When the glue has set overnight, attach the outer shell.

The curve of the front is made with strips that are individually beveled and fitted to create a smooth surface. Because the 1/4 in. plywood strips are only 1/2 in. wide, very little beveling, if any, is required. Once the glue has set completely, use a belt sander to smooth the strips to a smoothly curved surface.

As a point of information, although wood screws do not hold well in the edge grain of plywood, it is advisable to use screws when attaching solid stock, such as the supports and braces.

The molding along the back and lower edges of the outside body can be any pattern you like, the one shown being a hardwood purchased at a lumberyard. Some home centers might also have it, or something similar.

The skis are a straight grained, knot free hardwood such as ash, birch or oak. Ski thickness can be up to 1/2 in. if the forward 6 in. is reduced to about 5/16 in. before bending. The tips are placed in a 5 gallon can of boiling water and left for two hours. It may be necessary to add hot water during that time.

The form for bending the skis is made as detailed. Be sure to bore a hole to permit using a clamp through the 3/4 in. plywood backing of the bending jig. The backing also can be shaped from a scrap of 1 in. solid stock.

Keep the skis in the form for at least two days, then wait at least three days before applying any finish, to make sure the wood is thoroughly dry.

The "ironwork" is what may cause problems for some craftsmen, if they have not done this kind of work before. Half-inch square, hot rolled steel is used for the twisted legs that are welded to the runners and the flat steel supports that are screwed or bolted to the sled body. The runners could be 1/4 x 1 in. flat steel, although the legs should be 1/2 in. square, but need not be twisted.

A welding shop probably can shape and weld the runner assembly if you cannot handle this part of the project.

A triangular shape of 1/4 in. steel bar is welded to the fronts of the runners as indicated, and a metal ring is welded to the front of the triangle shape. This arrangement allows pulling the sleigh with a garden tractor or a large dog, if a proper harness is used. A cross country skier also could get in some training by pulling the sleigh, as it weighs only about 30 pounds, exclusive of the passenger.

For finishing, apply plastic upholstery material to the seat and back, then use a cushion when a passenger rides in the sleigh.

The completed sleigh can be stained and varnished, or painted. The runners are wire brushed, then painted flat black before being attached to the body. The shape of the runners does not have to exactly match those shown.

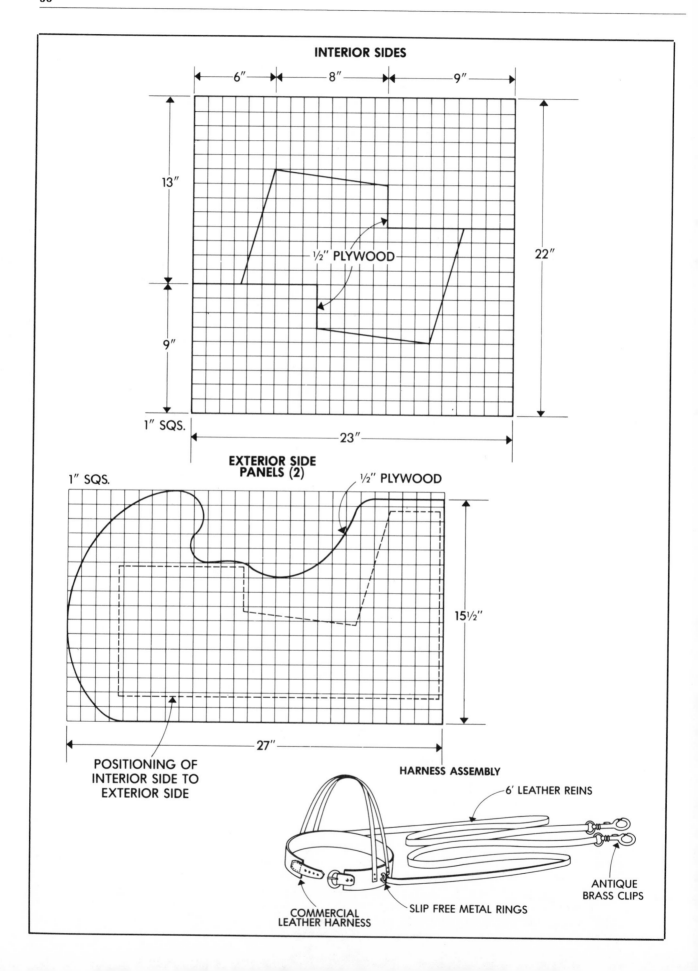

INTERIOR SIDES

6"   8"   9"

13"

½" PLYWOOD

22"

9"

1" SQS.

23"

EXTERIOR SIDE PANELS (2)

1" SQS.

½" PLYWOOD

15½"

27"

POSITIONING OF
INTERIOR SIDE TO
EXTERIOR SIDE

HARNESS ASSEMBLY

6' LEATHER REINS

ANTIQUE
BRASS CLIPS

COMMERCIAL
LEATHER HARNESS

SLIP FREE METAL RINGS

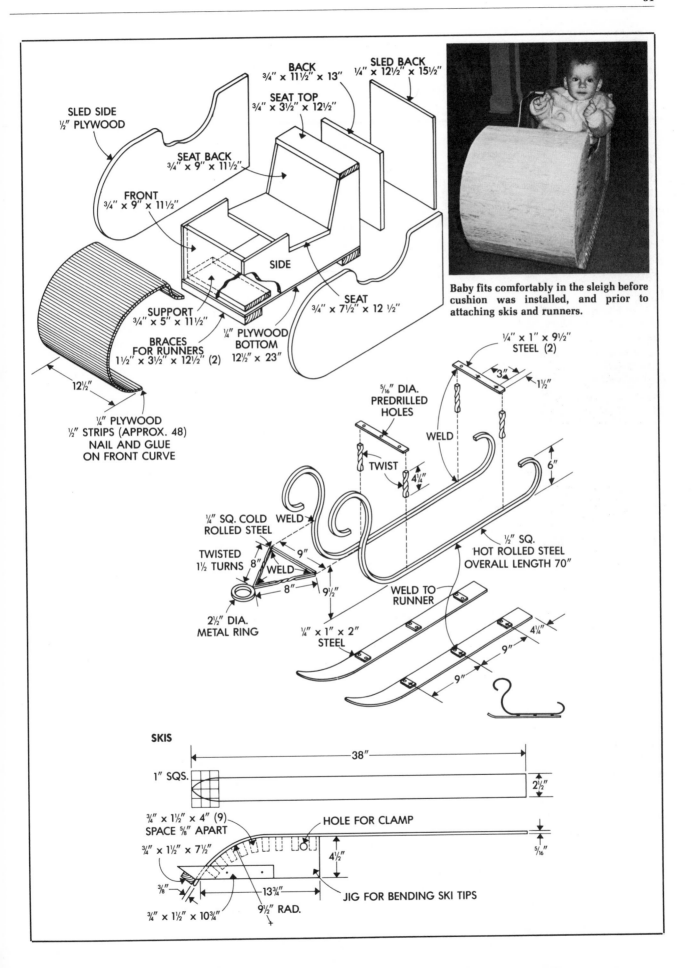

SLED SIDE
½" PLYWOOD

BACK
¾" × 11½" × 13"

SEAT TOP
¾" × 3½" × 12½"

SLED BACK
¼" × 12½" × 15½"

SEAT BACK
¾" × 9" × 11½"

FRONT
¾" × 9" × 11½"

SIDE

SUPPORT
¾" × 5" × 11½"

SEAT
¾" × 7½" × 12 ½"

BRACES
FOR RUNNERS
1½" × 3½" × 12½" (2)

¼" PLYWOOD
BOTTOM
12½" × 23"

12½"

¼" PLYWOOD
½" STRIPS (APPROX. 48)
NAIL AND GLUE
ON FRONT CURVE

Baby fits comfortably in the sleigh before cushion was installed, and prior to attaching skis and runners.

¼" × 1" × 9½"
STEEL (2)

3"

1½"

5/16" DIA.
PREDRILLED
HOLES

WELD

6"

TWIST

4¼"

¼" SQ. COLD
ROLLED STEEL

WELD

½" SQ.
HOT ROLLED STEEL
OVERALL LENGTH 70"

TWISTED
1½ TURNS

8"

9"

WELD

9½"

8"

WELD TO
RUNNER

2½" DIA.
METAL RING

¼" × 1" × 2"
STEEL

4¼"

9"

9"

SKIS

38"

1" SQS.

2½"

¾" × 1½" × 4" (9)
SPACE 5/8" APART

HOLE FOR CLAMP

5/16"

¾" × 1½" × 7½"

4½"

3/8"

13¾"

JIG FOR BENDING SKI TIPS

¾" × 1½" × 10¾"

9½" RAD.

Authentic Alaskan dog sled

Dog sleds are made in a variety of shapes and sizes and are used for hauling, for racing and other purposes. This seven foot sled is a composite design.

The sled is made mostly of birch with some oak used where extra strength is needed. The wood must be straight grained to provide the strength and resistance to breaking or cracking needed. Purchasing birch that already is planed is more expensive, but you have the advantage of selecting straight grained wood without knots or checks.

The runners are the most important part of the sled; they must be exactly straight and have the grain running in the same direction on both sides of the runners to prevent breaking when they are bent. Cut them from the straightest piece. Cut the false runners, stanchions, cross braces and basket slats from the next best wood. Cut and thickness plane all pieces before you start assembly. You probably should cut an extra runner and some extra basket slats as they sometimes split or break when being bent. Cut the stanchions and brush bow a little long, as they will be trimmed to fit.

First fit the two rear stanchions to the runners. The bottom ends of the stanchions are rounded to an oval shape and fitted into oval holes drilled in the runners. You can make a jig from stanchion material in which two 1 in. holes are drilled at an 85 degree angle. Material is cut out from between the holes to form a 1 x 2 in. oval hole. Use this jig to check the fit of

the stanchion ends and to mark the position of the holes drilled in the runners, as well as for a drill guide. The jig is clamped to the runner. Be careful not to alter the angle of the hole while drilling. Be sure to back up all pieces being drilled with some scrap wood so the bit will make a clean exit.

Drill the holes for stanchions No. 2 and No. 3 before the runners are bent. Delay drilling the hole for stanchion No. 1 until after the runners are bent to preclude breakage at the hole. Stanchion No. 1 should be placed directly in back of the bend of the runner with No. 2 spaced evenly between No. 1 and No. 3. Allow about 24 in. from the rear of stanchion No. 3 and the end of the runner.

A fixture for bending runners, slats and top rail is shown in the drawing. Pine boards can be used to make a form with the proper shape which measures about 4-1/2 in. wide. Gussets are attached to the front and rear of the form. The rear gusset extends 3 in. above the form so a 3/4 in. dowel can be inserted.

A steamer can consist of an oil drum with holes cut in each end and a vent hole cut in the top. Keep it about 2/3 filled with water and place it on cinder blocks over a charcoal and wood fire.

A good procedure for bending the runners, slats and top rail is as follows: The wood is soaked overnight in hot water. Pieces then are placed in the steamer for a minimum of two hours. Rags are stuffed in the holes on either end.

Excess steam escapes through the vent hole. After the boards are removed from the steamer they are kept wrapped in hot cloths soaked in boiling water. Both runners are bent at the same time. The noses of the runners are placed at the front of the form and clamped. Blocks of 1 x 2 stock are placed between all the clamps and the runners. Runners are slowly bent until they can be clamped at position X1. They again are soaked with boiling water and rags, then bent and clamped at position X2. This is repeated until they can be clamped at position X3. A dowel is inserted in the rear gusset and wedges driven between it and the runners. Soak the runners at the bend for another 15 minutes and then set them aside to dry for 10 days.

The slats and top rail are bent in the same manner. It's too difficult to try to bend more than two or three slats at one time. With a wider fixture you possibly could do all at one time, two layers of four each. Slats are thinner and are easier to bend. They need to stay in the fixture for only a week. But keep them clamped to maintain the bend until they are used.

After the runners are bent, complete the installation of the stanchions. Use a protractor to set the angle. The front stanchion is set at 85 degrees, the other two at 87 degrees. They are pinned with 1/4 in. dowels. A drill guide is helpful in drilling perfectly aligned holes for pinning the runners.

Four of the cross braces have turned ends that are pegged to the stanchions. Turn these in a lathe, then sand them for a final fit. Allow them to protrude through the stanchions about 1/4 in., then after they are drilled and pinned with 1/4 in. dowels, cut them off flush with the stanchions. Mark and number each cross brace and stanchion fitting, as they are each a custom fit.

The cross brace height determines the height of the basket which can vary depending on the type of terrain where the sled will be used. The top of the cross brace can be as low as 6 in. above the false runner. This one is 8-1/2 in. to give a ground clearance of about 10 in. The upper cross brace on the rear stanchion is located 14-1/2 in. above the lower cross brace.

The two outside basket slats are bolted on the front to the nose piece and runners. The nose piece is wedge shaped so as to fit between the runners and the outer slats. The outer slats also are notched to fit even with the outside of the stanchions. Temporarily fit the runners, nose piece and outer slats to locate the exact position of the notches. When cutting the notches allow a little extra depth in the notch to provide flexibility.

The overall width of the basket is 19-1/2 in. The inner slats are spaced evenly between the larger outer slats, which means there is slightly over an inch of spacing. Bolt the slats to the nose piece using 1/4 in. carriage bolts. The outer slats have the head on the bottom next to the runner. Be sure to use a washer under the nuts. Cut off the outer bolts even with the nut and peen slightly to prevent loosening. The bolts of the inner slats are mounted with the head on top of the slats to provide a smooth surface in the basket.

The slats are fastened to the cross braces with countersunk No. 7 x 1-1/4 in. flathead wood screws. Drill pilot holes and wax the screws to prevent splitting the wood. The point where the slat touches the cross brace is called a bench. The cross brace should be planed so all of its surface touches the slat, not just the leading edge. A fifth cross brace is positioned about 9 in. in front of the front

stanchion, screwed to the slats to provide extra support to the front of the basket.

The false runners provide additional strength to the runners but they do not need to be bent. They are cut so they fit the stanchions and can slide over the runner from the outside. Bolt them to the runners with 1/4 x 1 in. carriage bolts with the head on top of the false runner and the nuts counterbored so they do not protrude past the bottom surface of the runners. Put one bolt in front of No. 1 stanchion, one between stanchions No. 1 and No. 2, and a third between stanchions No. 2 and No. 3. The foot pad, to be added later, will secure the rear of the top and bottom runners.

Position the top rail so it fits on top of the stanchions. It should fit so the bend ends just in front of stanchion No. 1 and continues to have a slight curve up to stanchion No. 3. There should be a slight pull at the center stanchion. Trim the stanchions to fit. The middle stanchion will probably need to be shorter than the 24 in. shown in the drawing. It also may be necessary to cut off some of the rear of the top rail so that it's even with the rear of stanchion No. 3. The top rail can be screwed to the stanchions with No. 7 x 1-1/4 in. flathead screws and laced through 1/2 in. holes drilled in the stanchions. The front of the top rail is laced to the outer basket slat.

The hand rail and brush bow are made of strips of 1/8 in. birch. Use a form with an 11 in. radius as shown. After cutting the strips clamp them to the form with clamps using plenty of glue, two layers at a time, until they are built up to 7/8 in. Let them dry for two days in the form, then sand them. The handle has a section reduced in width for a handhold. Cut this with a saw before the strips are glued together.

The handrail is positioned so the curve is just outside the rear stanchions. It fits under the top rails and ends at an angle butted against the rear of the middle stanchion. It will be necessary to cut it to fit. Lacing holds it in place. After the sled has been varnished, wrap the

handgrip with tape.

The brush bow is laced to the nose piece and through holes to the front stanchion. Cut the ends of the bow at an angle parallel with the runners. For added strength, add to the brush bow a length of 1/4 in. oak three-fourths the length of the bow and lace it to the inside before mounting the brush bow to the sled.

Mount the foot pads to the runners with counterbored carriage bolts. Ribbed rubber is glued to the top of the foot pads which will cover the heads of the bolts.

Stanchions are further strengthened by lacing them to screw eyes centered in the top runner and about 3 in. to the front and rear of the stanchions. Lacing is through a hole in the stanchion about 4 in. above the runner.

A 2 in. wide strip of 1/4 or 1/2 in. thick plastic is fastened to the bottom of the runner. Make sure there are no bolts protruding below the bottom of the runner, then screw the plastic to the runner with No. 7 x 5/8 in. counterbored flathead screws spaced about 10 in. apart.

The brake is made of 3/8 in. steel rod. You can have this made at a welding shop. It is fastened to the brake board with a U-bolt and eye bolts. The brake board is loosely laced to the nose piece through two 1/2 in. holes spaced about 2 in. apart. It is held up at the rear with two springs which can be door springs fastened to the eye bolts with S hooks and at the sides to the handrails with lacing.

Extra holes in the stanchions are used for 3/8 in. rope which is laced in an X or Y pattern to form a basket to hold cargo or a person. It crisscrosses between the rear stanchions.

Varnish the sled with two coats of polyurethane or spar varnish. It may need additional coats of varnish before each sledding season.

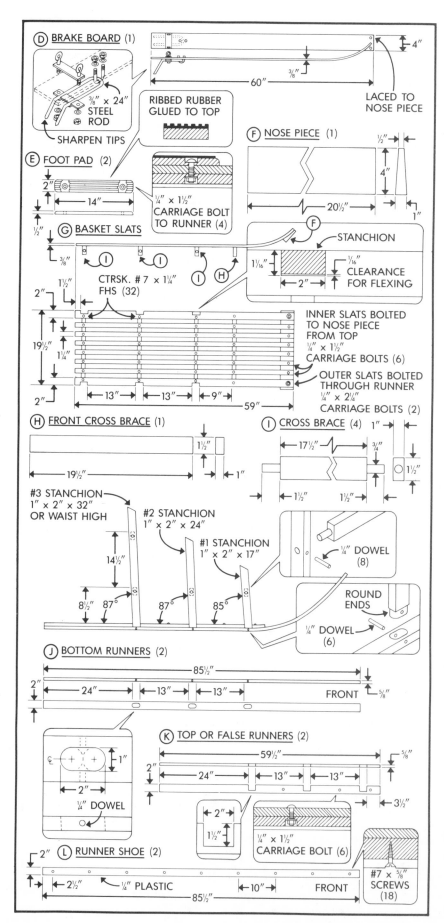

(D) BRAKE BOARD (1)

4"

3/8"

60"

LACED TO
NOSE PIECE

3/8" × 24"
STEEL
ROD

SHARPEN TIPS

RIBBED RUBBER
GLUED TO TOP

(F) NOSE PIECE (1)

1/2"

4"

20½"

1"

(E) FOOT PAD (2)

2"

14"

1/2"

1/4" × 1½"
CARRIAGE BOLT
TO RUNNER (4)

(F) STANCHION

1 1/16"

2"

1/16"

CLEARANCE
FOR FLEXING

(G) BASKET SLATS

3/8"

(I)   (I)   (I)   (H)

CTRSK. # 7 × 1¼"
FHS (32)

1½"

2"

1¼"

19½"

2"

13"   13"   9"

59"

INNER SLATS BOLTED
TO NOSE PIECE
FROM TOP
1/4" × 1½"
CARRIAGE BOLTS (6)

OUTER SLATS BOLTED
THROUGH RUNNER
1/4" × 2¼"
CARRIAGE BOLTS (2)

(H) FRONT CROSS BRACE (1)

1½"

19½"

1"

(I) CROSS BRACE (4)

1"

17½"

3/4"

1½"

1½"   1½"

#3 STANCHION
1" × 2" × 32"
OR WAIST HIGH

#2 STANCHION
1" × 2" × 24"

#1 STANCHION
1" × 2" × 17"

1/4" DOWEL
(8)

14½"

8½"   87°

87°   85°

ROUND
ENDS

1/4" DOWEL
(6)

(J) BOTTOM RUNNERS (2)

85½"

2"

24"   13"   13"

FRONT

5/8"

1"

2"

1/4" DOWEL

(K) TOP OR FALSE RUNNERS (2)

59½"

5/8"

2"

24"   13"   13"

3½"

2"

1½"

1/4" × 1½"
CARRIAGE BOLT (6)

#7 × 5/8"
SCREWS
(18)

(L) RUNNER SHOE (2)

2"

2½"   1/4" PLASTIC   10"   FRONT

85½"

Back view shows brake board in down
position. Brake is not installed nor are
springs fastened to handrail.

Side view of form used to bend runners,
slats and top rail. Rear gusset has dowel
that supports wedge block.

Form for bending runners (left); gluing
form for handrail and brush bow (right
rear); jig for fitting stanchions.

55

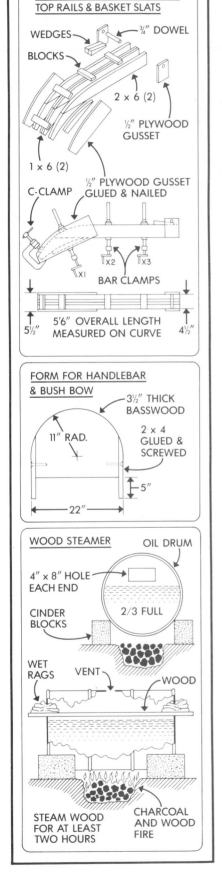

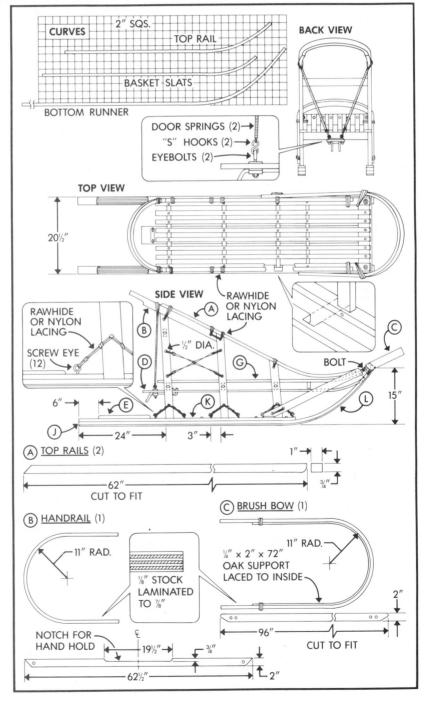

FORM FOR BOTTOM RUNNERS, TOP RAILS & BASKET SLATS

WEDGES
BLOCKS
3/4" DOWEL
2 x 6 (2)
1/2" PLYWOOD GUSSET
1 x 6 (2)
C-CLAMP
1/2" PLYWOOD GUSSET GLUED & NAILED
X1
X2 X3
BAR CLAMPS
5 1/2"
5'6" OVERALL LENGTH MEASURED ON CURVE
4 1/2"

FORM FOR HANDLEBAR & BUSH BOW

3 1/2" THICK BASSWOOD
11" RAD.
2 x 4 GLUED & SCREWED
5"
22"

WOOD STEAMER

OIL DRUM
4" x 8" HOLE EACH END
CINDER BLOCKS
2/3 FULL
WET RAGS
VENT
WOOD
STEAM WOOD FOR AT LEAST TWO HOURS
CHARCOAL AND WOOD FIRE

MATERIALS LIST

Birch
 2 x 8 x 8' (1)
 2 x 6 x 8' (1)
 1 x 8 x 8' (1)
 2 x 4 x 4' (1)
White oak
 1 x 6 x 5' (1)
1/4" x 36" birch dowel (2)
1/4" x 2" x 8' white plastic (2)
1/2" diameter screw eye (12)
Carriage bolts
 1/4" x 1" (8)
 1/4" x 1-1/2" (10)
 1/4" x 2-1/4" (2)

Plated flathead wood screws
 #7 x 5/8" (18)
 #7 x 1-1/4" (32)
Door springs (2)
S hooks (2)
Eyebolt, 1/4" x 1-1/2" (2)
U-bolt, 1/4" x 1-1/2" (1)
3/8" x 24" steel rod
Numerous pieces of rawhide or nylon tuna leader (solid diamond core)
3/8" nylon water skiing rope to lace basket
Polyurethane or spar varnish

CURVES 2" SQS. TOP RAIL BACK VIEW
BASKET SLATS
BOTTOM RUNNER
DOOR SPRINGS (2)
"S" HOOKS (2)
EYEBOLTS (2)
TOP VIEW
20 1/2"
RAWHIDE OR NYLON LACING
SIDE VIEW
RAWHIDE OR NYLON LACING
SCREW EYE (12)
1/2" DIA.
BOLT
6"
24" 3"
15"
(A) TOP RAILS (2)
1" 3/4"
62" CUT TO FIT
(B) HANDRAIL (1)
11" RAD.
1/8" STOCK LAMINATED TO 7/8"
NOTCH FOR HAND HOLD
19 1/2" 3/4"
62 1/2" 2"
(C) BRUSH BOW (1)
11" RAD.
1/4" x 2" x 72" OAK SUPPORT LACED TO INSIDE
96" CUT TO FIT
2"

Dinky duck boat

Simple enough even for talented youngsters to build, yet sturdy and lightweight so it can be used as a utility boat, this little craft is a fun boat for both children and adults. The removable open top cabin is optional and serves as a splash guard as well as adding to the appearance. Materials needed are standard dimension lumber and one sheet of 1/4 in. marine plywood.

To begin construction, cut the bow beam and transom to size. Cut the sides to 96 in. and fasten to the bow and transom using waterproof glue and flathead wood screws. Cut off the rear projections of the sides to match the angle of the transom. Mark the position of the front lower edge of the bow on the outer surface of the sides. Bend a thin piece of wood into a gentle curve and starting at the mark, draw along the wood to the lower edge of the side, about 12 in. back. Trace this pattern and repeat on the opposite side. Cut off both sides using a coping or saber saw. Cut and install the three 2 x 2 cross members, again using waterproof glue and screws. Turn the framing upside down and plane and sand all edges, checking with a straight-edge to make sure they will receive

the bottom snugly.

Wrap the 1/4 in. plywood in wet burlap overnight to make it bendable. Using No. 11 flathead wood screws and waterproof glue, fasten the plywood to the bow. Gradually bend over the curve and drive No. 8 screws, 1 in. apart, into the sides as you proceed toward the transom. Make the three lift-off seats as shown.

Assemble the cabin; it fits down between the sides, resting on molding. The windshield is simply a frame with clear sheet plastic set in sawn slots. If the boat is used by adults, make a grating of 1 x 1s to fasten over the 2 x 2 cross members. This distributes the weight more evenly over the thin bottom. Sand smooth and paint the boat inside and out with two coats.

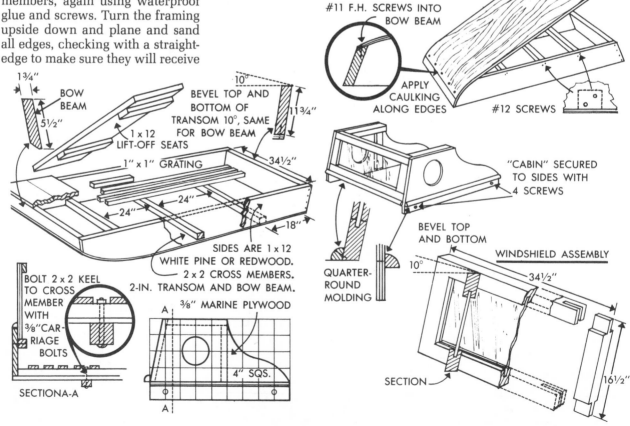

Pelican Pull Toy

Toddlers will be enchanted with this friendly pull toy that "talks" as they pull him along, a simple wire linkage opening and closing his voluminous beak. All parts of the toy can be made from scraps of wood you probably have in your shop.

The base is 3/4 in. plywood or 1 in. solid stock, the body is 1/2 or 3/4 in. material and the wings and beak halves are 1/4 in. stock. Make cardboard patterns of the various pieces from the squared drawings, then saw out the shapes.

If you have no lathe for turning the wheels, first draw them on your stock and saw them out slightly oversize. Bore a hole through the center of each wheel, slip a nut and

bolt through the hole and chuck it in a drill press or variable speed drill and "turn" each wheel to size with a rasp, file and sandpaper on a block of wood.

The linkage is formed from coat hanger wire, while the front axle can be slightly heavier wire or a long nail. The rear axles are No. 8 x 1-1/2 in. flathead wood screws countersunk into the wheel.

The only part of the toy that may present problems is the linkage. If the beak does not move freely, move it forward slightly; the brads used will not make large holes and can be tapped in lightly before checking the operation. When the beak works freely, tap them in all the way.

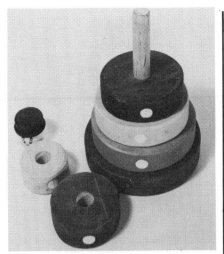

Stacking Ring Clown

Very often the most simple toy is the best one. This toddler's stacking toy is a case in point. It is simply disks of wood cut from 1-1/4 in. softwood. Each disk has a 3/4 in. hole bored in the center that then is sanded to provide an easy sliding fit on a 3/4 in. dowel.

The several disks, as shown in the drawing, stack on the dowel that is glued into the bottom disk.

The head of the clown is turned on a lathe and sanded smooth. A 3/4 in. blind hole is drilled in the bottom of the head so it will fit over the top of the dowel. Be sure the clown head is not so small it could be swallowed by a child.

Also be sure the enamel you use is nontoxic and safe for children. If you paint the dowel, be sure the holes in the disks still slip easily over the dowel.

Glue a piece of felt or cork to the underside of the bottom disk to protect surfaces on which the clown is placed.

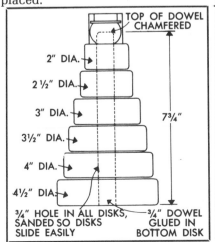

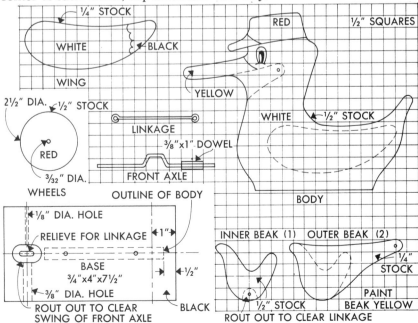

Walking Bunny

The lifelike action of this "walking bunny" will captivate both young and old, and it can be built in an hour or so with a few pieces of scrap wood.

Use 1/2 to 3/4 in. wood of close and uniform grain. Uniformity of the wood density and weight is essential for good balance. Cut around the pattern lines with either a jig saw or coping saw, then drill the 3/8 in. holes in the body and legs.

To assemble, glue dowels in one leg, put a washer on the pivoting dowel, add the body and a second washer, rub glue on ends of dowels and push on second leg. Avoid using excess glue. Before glue sets assure proper clearance between legs and body for action.

If you wish to paint the bunny, do so before assembling. Place the bunny on an inclined board and he will walk down it all by himself with a "determined" gait.

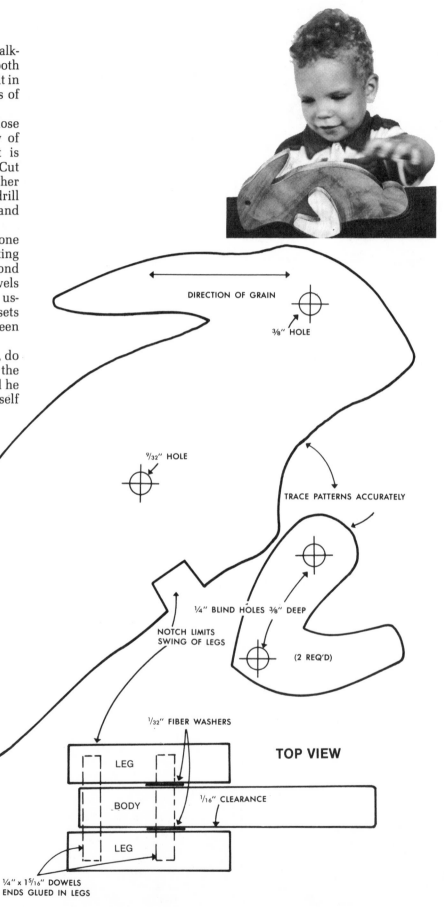

DIRECTION OF GRAIN

⅜" HOLE

⁹⁄₃₂" HOLE

TRACE PATTERNS ACCURATELY

¼" BLIND HOLES ⅜" DEEP

NOTCH LIMITS SWING OF LEGS

(2 REQ'D)

¹⁄₃₂" FIBER WASHERS

TOP VIEW

LEG

BODY

¹⁄₁₆" CLEARANCE

LEG

¼" x 1⁵⁄₁₆" DOWELS ENDS GLUED IN LEGS

Stacking Wagon Pull Toy

This popular toy teaches coordination and recognition of visual relationships as the child plays with it—and most importantly, it's fun for the child to assemble.

Hardwoods (recommended), softwoods or a combination of the two can be used. This is an ideal project for cleaning up your shop scrap pile.

We suggest that you gather the various pieces of different woods before you begin cutting. Assign shapes to the individual pieces of different woods according to the sizes of the stock available and the graining.

The fundamental dimension is 3-1/2 in. The square pieces are 3-1/2 in. on each side and the sanded doughnut wheels are 3-1/2 in. in diameter. The rectangular pieces with two holes are 3-1/2 x 7 in. and the main runners are 3-1/2 x 14 in. (holes 3-1/2 in. apart).

The two center holes in the runners have dowels glued into them. Use 7/8 or 1 in. dowels; determine height according to thickness of other component pieces.

The end holes in the runners slip over dowels glued vertically into the axles. The axles themselves are made of 1-1/2 in. square maple, with the ends turned a bit under 1 in. to accept the wheels. Smaller 3/8 in. dowels are used as keeper pins to hold the wheels in place on the axle.

All edges, especially those on exposed dowel ends, should be sanded and smoothed completely. Add the tow rope and handle (1 in. dowel) and the toy is ready for finishing. Use a good nontoxic sealer and varnish to complete your work.

Disassembled toy looks more complicated than it really is. Uniformity of dimensions simplifies construction.

First step in assembly clarifies entire procedure, helps child visualize relationship between pieces and final goal.

Lacing Boot Bank

Here's a one-evening project that can be duplicated dozens of times once the first pattern is made. It is a good gift shop item for a craftsman who wants to make a few dollars from his hobby, because in addition to being a handsome bank, it has the practical educational aspect as an aid to teaching a child to lace and tie shoes.

Scraps of almost any kind of wood can be used, since the finished project is painted. The one pictured was painted a bright red with white lacing. The latter can be an actual shoelace, heavy twine or yarn in a color that contrasts with that of the boot.

Enlarge the squared drawing to make patterns for the sides, and the edges of the front and back. Use stiff cardboard for the patterns, or even 1/8 in. hardboard if you want to use the patterns to make several banks.

A band saw does the job quickly, but an electric jig saw or even a hand scroll saw can be used to cut the profiles. Be sure to slightly round all cut edges with sandpaper to remove any roughness or splinters.

If you can't find corks for the hole in the bottom through which the money is recovered, bore a hole that is a snug fit for a short length of 1 in. dowel.

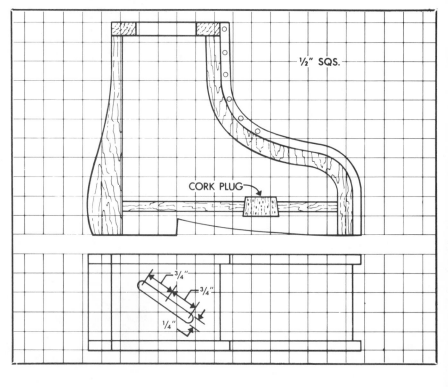

Tiny Tot's Rocking Horse

For some reason tiny tots will spend more time rocking than at practically any other form of play. This cartoonish little happy horse is sure to capture a little one's affections.

The first step in construction is to enlarge the squared drawings to make your patterns, then cut out the seat board, two runners and the head. If you use solid stock, be sure the grain runs the length of the several pieces to assure maximum strength. When softwood is used for the seat and runners, it's a good idea to use plywood for the horse head.

Use a coping saw, saber or band saw to cut the pieces, clamping the rockers together so they will be identical.

Sand all pieces thoroughly, using progressively finer grits to achieve a glass-smooth surface. Next, assemble the sanded rockers and seat board with glue and screws. Fasten the brace between the rockers, flush with the front of the seat board.

Leave the horse head off for the moment and apply a generous coat or two of sealer to the head and partly assembled rocker. Be sure the sealer and other finishing materials are nontoxic and "child-safe." Toddlers often chew on toys.

After the sealer has dried, paint on the eyes, mane and ears. Use black paint or a black felt-tip pen. The halter is bright red. When the patterns are dry, apply another coat of clear sealer.

When the sealer is dry, attach the head to the rocker with glue and screws. Bore the 5/8 in. hole and glue in the 5 in. length of dowel. Be sure to wipe away excess glue.

When the glue has set, apply several more coats of clear nontoxic sealer, sanding between each coat.

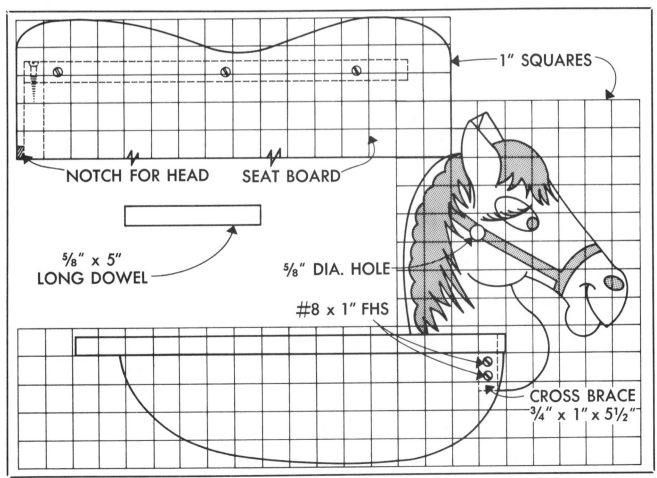

Even the smallest buckeroo will enjoy this old time "merry-go-round" horse. It actually is nothing more than a sturdy seat with rockers. A dowel is used both as a handhold for the child, and to keep him safely in place.

Additionally, a leather strap could be run from the center of the dowel, down to the center of the underside of the seat to prevent the child from sliding down and out.

The two sides are cut from 3/4 in. hardwood plywood. Make a pattern by enlarging the squared drawing, and be sure to mark the locations for the dowels, screws, seat and footboards.

Note that the handhold dowel and the stretcher dowels require blind holes 1/4 in. deep on the inside surfaces of the sides. A countersunk hole is bored from the outside surfaces of the sides so screws can be driven into the centers of the dowels. Similar holes are drilled for the screws that hold the seat and back.

Cut out the sides and bore the necessary holes. Sand all edges carefully, and fill any voids or rough spots. Final-sand, then paint both sides white. Be sure the paint you use for any part of the project is nontoxic.

While the paint on the sides is drying, cut the seat, back and footboard from 1/2 in. stock. Use 3/4 in. plywood for the seat, or use lighter stock if you prefer to keep down the weight of the rocker.

Fasten the seat and back together with glue and screws.

The handhold dowel is cut from 3/4 in. dowel, the length of the seat and footboard, plus 1/2 in. for the two 1/4 in. deep blind holes. The two bottom 1/2 in. stretchers are cut exactly the same length.

Paint the seat/back assembly, the footboard and the two bottom stretcher dowels a bright red. Leave the handhold dowel unfinished, but sand it as smooth as possible. The handhold dowel is the one the toddler might use for teething.

Go back to the white-painted side pieces and mark out the pattern for the horses. Paint the rockers, saddle and bridle with red; the mane, tail, eyes and trim are black.

Toddler Rocking Horse Chair

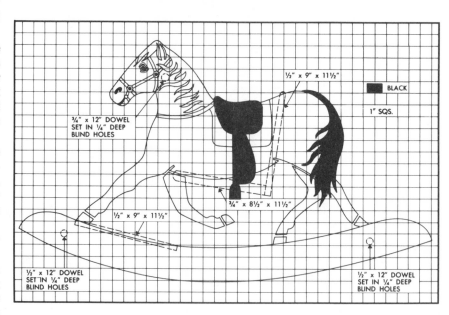

Assembling all the pieces can be a bit tricky, so an assistant would be very helpful. Place one side down on a padded surface, outside down, insert the several dowels with glue and position the footboard and seat.

You may be able to fit the other side onto the projecting dowels, and over the seat assembly and footboard, but it might be easier to turn the assembly over and fit it into the other side that is placed inside up on a padded surface.

Drive screws into the dowels, and into the seat and footboard. It's a good idea to mark the positions of the seat and footboard on the painted surfaces to aid in positioning them.

Invert the assembly, and drive screws through from the outside of the other side, being careful to get the seat and footboard in their proper positions.

Clean off any excess glue and touch up any flaws in the paint created while driving screws.

Rocking Zebra

There are lots of rocking horses around, but the kid with the zebra is the envy of all his friends. And you'll get extra applause for building one (or you can make it a horse or pony from the same plan).

Hardly perceptible except to the experienced eye is a safety feature on the rockers themselves. Continuous arc rockers are fine for toddlers, but when an older child kicks the zebra into too hard a gallop it would be possible to rock completely over, either foward or backward.

For that reason the ends of the rockers are turned slightly down at the back and front to retard the rockers' travel. This would not, of course, prevent a child from being thrown forward or backward off the zebra if he or she was too rambunctious.

The rockers are made by striking off an arc with a radius of 33 in. for the outside curve and 31 in. for the inside curve to create rockers 2 in. high. The downward turn begins about 1-1/2 squares in from each end. The greater the downward curve, the better the snubbing action. Glue two pieces of 3/4 in. plywood together to make the stock. A straight-line measurement between the tips of the rockers measures 42 in. The idle zebra tilts forward slightly, but levels when a child gets aboard.

Note that dowels should run completely across between the rockers and through the legs, although they are not shown in the photo.

The black and white paint job makes the zebra. Merely alter the paint job to make a pinto, a dapple or some other colored horse.

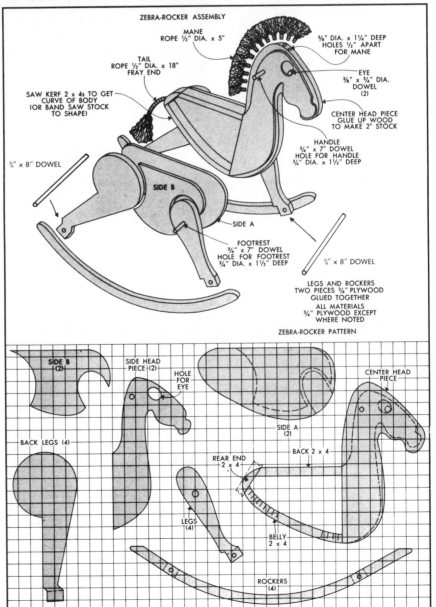

Two-Way Tot's Teeter/Slide

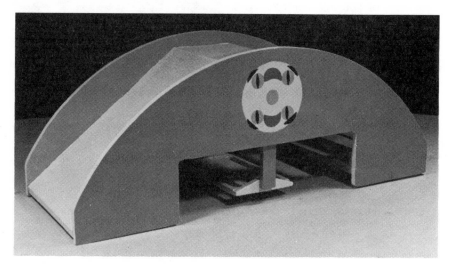

Here's an indoor/outdoor toy that is sure to provide hours of fun for the little ones the year 'round. Designed especially for toddlers, the teeter/slide is exactly what its name implies. With the curved side down, children can enjoy rocking back and forth, just like on a teeter-totter. With the curved side up, it becomes a slide, complete with ladder and hand rails. Since the teeter/slide is made of exterior-grade plywood and painted with enamel, there is no need to worry when it is left out in bad weather. If it should become muddy and the youngsters want to bring it into the house, it is easily cleaned with the garden hose.

Begin by marking a 27-1/2 in. radius for the side panels on a piece of 3/4 in. plywood. A compass can be fashioned out of a piece of string, a tack and a pencil. Tie the pencil to one end of the string, then tack the string, with the proper length for the radius, to the edge of the plywood on the centerline. Draw the arc, checking that the squared ends of the panel are the same. Now mark the "step-through," following the dimensions given in the drawing. Tack nail the marked piece to the piece to be used for the other side panel. The profiles can now be sawed. Clamp the pieces in a vise and smooth the edges until both pieces are identical.

Using 1/2 in. plywood, cut pieces for the ladder and slide to the dimensions given in the drawing. Now you are ready to cut the steps for the ladder. First mark the step locations and 1/2 in. radii. Using a 1 in. bit, bore the corners at each center point used to mark the radii. You can now cut out the steps. Round the edges of the steps with a file or a rounding over bit in a portable router.

Next, cut the seats, bottom panel and handle to the dimensions given. Set the blade of a power saw at 53 and 90 degrees and cut angles on the front and back edge of both seats. The "grips" on the handle are made by boring 1 in. holes at the end of each marked slot and sawing out the remainder. After the handle is cut, round all edges smooth.

Complete making the parts by cutting the handle posts and other various brackets to the dimensions given.

Start assembly by gluing and screwing the seat brackets (D) into position on the side panels. Add the panel brackets (B) and bottom panel bracket (C), making sure the bottom panel bracket is centered on the vertical centerline. Now glue and screw the handle posts into position.

With the side panels on edge, curved side up, attach the bottom panel. Now, run a bead of glue along the panel brackets and position the slide and ladder. Tap them snug against the bottom panel and counterbore holes in the locations shown. Secure the slide and ladder with screws, driving the screws deep enough so they can be filled.

Next attach the seats. Make sure that the front edge of each seat is flush with the side panels before installing permanently.

Lastly, secure the handle brackets to the handle using No. 6 x 1-1/4 in. roundhead screws. Now position and attach the assembly to the handle posts.

Fill and sand all edges and surfaces smooth, then apply a coat of sealer. When dry, lightly sand and paint the teeter/slide with colors of your choice. Give the slide several coats, sanding between coats to produce a smooth finish. After the paint has dried, you can paint the clown face. If you prefer, use large decals that are available at paint and wallpaper stores.

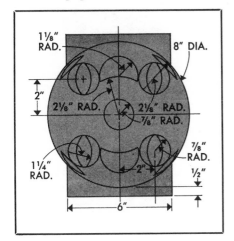

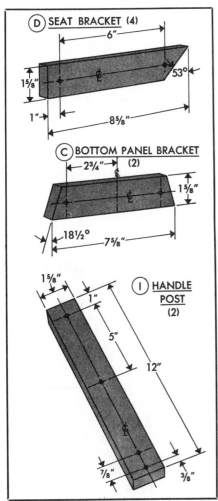

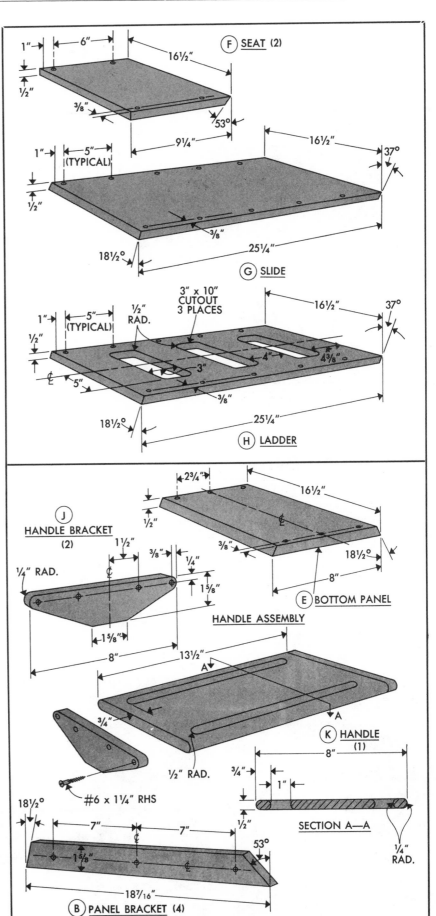

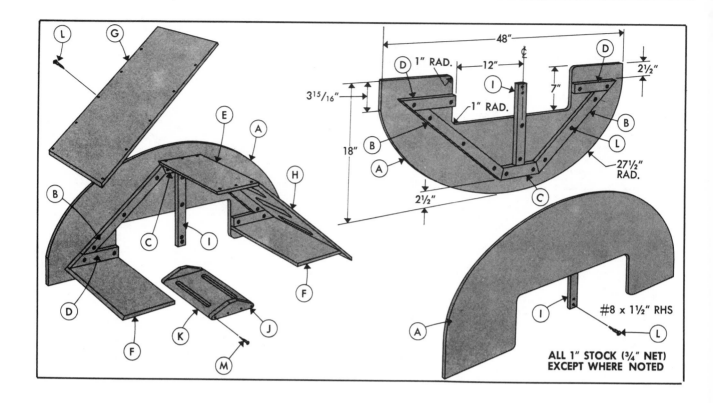

Little Red Barn

Most children like to play with toy animals, and if you have any young "farmers" in your family, this little old-fashioned barn might be just what they want for their "livestock."

The barn shown is a bit less than 10 x 12 in. in floor area, which is alright for smallish toy animals, but if the ones your children have are large, increase the size of the barn proportionately.

The barn shown was assembled from 1 x 12 shelving stock, which generally is quite straight-grained and clear. There is no reason why you couldn't use scraps of other kinds of wood you may have in the shop.

The roof is cut from 1/4 in. hardboard, but you might prefer plywood, or even solid stock. Scraps of wall paneling also would be suitable. If you made several barns as

gifts, it would be a good way to use up those wood scraps that seem to collect in the shop, but never get used.

The stall and ladder are made by ripping 1/4 x 1/4 in. strips, then joining them with popsicle sticks that you can purchase at hobby shops. Alternately, simply rip thin strips to about 1/8 in. thick and use them.

If the barn is made larger than the one dimensioned here, the stock for

the ladder and stall should be heavier than that shown in the drawing.

The stall and ladder are assembled with glue, no brads or nails being used. This eliminates the chance of snagging tiny fingers on nail or brad points.

Paint the barn bright red with a white roof. White is used to frame the door and simulate a sliding door, as indicated. White also is used for the windows painted on the ends of the barn. For a more realistic look, you might use strips of thin wood, as used for the ladder treads and stall, to frame the windows and door.

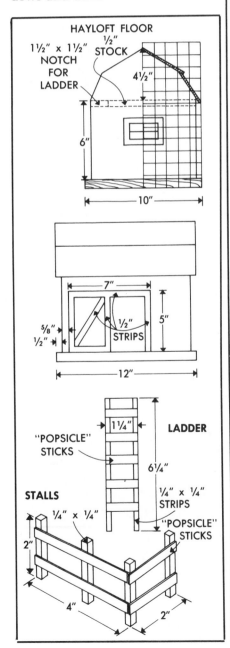

Miniature Wooden Toy Cars

Wooden toys have ageless appeal. They are fun and easy to make, children delight in playing with them, and they offer a refreshing change from their fragile plastic counterparts—well-crafted wooden toys should last a family through several generations of active use.

The toys shown here were built using two basic construction methods. The Volkswagen, van and station wagon were built from blocks of 4 x 4, with plywood bumpers and wheels added. The other vehicles were built up from 3/4 in. stock with various pieces added as shown.

Beginning toymakers sometimes are perplexed by the question of wheel making techniques. The wheels shown on these vehicles can be made any of several ways.

If large diameter dowels are available, you can slice off the wheels as required. If suitable doweling is unavailable in your area and you do not have a lathe, you may be able to have dowels turned at a nominal charge by a local cabinetmaker.

Another approach is to cut wood or plywood disks, using a fly-cutter or hole saw in a drill press. A hole saw in a portable drill will do an acceptable job.

If you do not have the materials, tools or desire to make wheels yourself, you can buy them. Purchased wheels will be slightly thicker than the plywood ones used here, but you can sand them to the desired thickness.

To make any of the 4 x 4 block-based toys, the first step is to cut the body to overall length. Next, cut the various side and top profiles shown. Cut the wheel-well arcs with a hole saw and use a chisel to cut away the scrap, or bore the wheel wells to exact depth and diameter (an expansive bit can be a real convenience for such jobs).

Drill axle holes in the wheels and body, then insert 3/8 in. dowel axles. The holes for the axles should be slightly oversize, and the axle centers should be lightly waxed to assure smooth turning. Mount washers as spacers outside the body on the axles and glue the wheels on the axle ends.

To make the built-up vehicles, cut the necessary components for each and mark the pieces for identification. Assembly is straight glue and clamp, but we do recommend that you assemble the center sections first, working from the bottom up. Follow the same wheel mounting procedures as for the 4 x 4 toys.

All wooden toys should be thoroughly sanded, with particular attention given to the corners and edges. If you want the bright colors and protection offered by enamel, be sure to select a child-safe, non-toxic type.

Here are a few tips on construction of the individual toys:

Volkswagen. Cut a slanted kerf for the windshield (lower edge approximately 1-1/2 in. from the front edge of the body) before cutting the curved and slanted profiles.

Van/Bus. Cut the slanted sides (window areas), then cut the front.

Station Wagon. Cut the side window areas, kerf for the windshield, then complete the front "notch" by cutting across the hood area.

Semi-Tractor and Trailer. Make the trailer first, then cut and assemble all the tractor except the pivot block for the trailer. Place the trailer's hitch in the pivot block, hold the block in place on the tractor, and move the trailer from side to side; the front of the trailer should clear the back of the cab. If the pivot action is unrestricted, attach the block as shown; otherwise, move the block back as required or cut and drill another one to fit.

Jeep. To simplify assembly, you can modify the plans to provide for a folded-down windshield.

Pickup Truck and Camper. If you have any true 4 x 4 in. (net) stock, you can use it for a closed camper to simplify construction design.

Jeep is as distinctive as Volkswagen; "peg people" can have green helmets and uniforms for a military version.

Van/bus has slightly-angled side window areas; for a more emphatic and readily identifiable look, paint on "windows."

Volkswagen's shape is ideal for a wooden toy—a distinctive profile incorporating swept, curved lines.

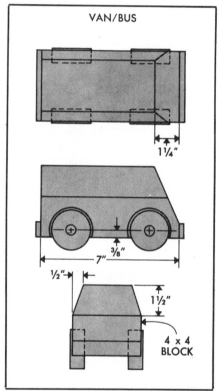

VAN/BUS

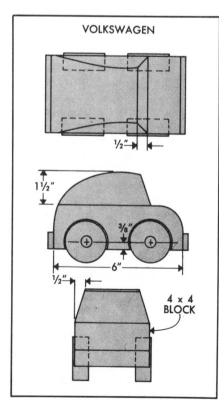

VOLKSWAGEN

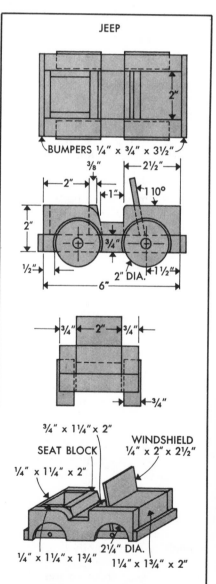

JEEP

Station wagon can be heightened to give panel truck appearance, or raised with a base block for 4-wheel drive look.

STATION WAGON

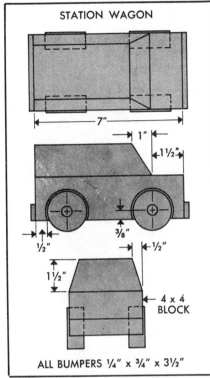

7"

1"

1½"

⅜"

½"

½"

1½"

4 x 4 BLOCK

ALL BUMPERS ¼" x ¾" x 3½"

Tractor-trailer combination has the powerful, husky look of the real thing.

SEMI TRAILER

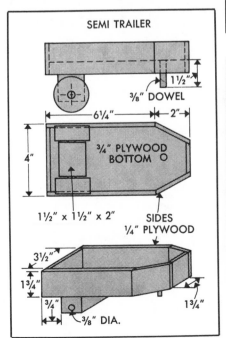

1½"

⅜" DOWEL

6¼"

2"

4"

¾" PLYWOOD BOTTOM

1½" x 1½" x 2"

SIDES ¼" PLYWOOD

3½"

1¾"

¾"

1¾"

⅜" DIA.

SEMI TRACTOR

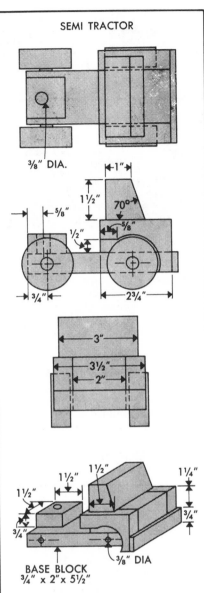

⅜" DIA.

1"

1½"

70°

⅝"

½"

⅝"

¾"

2¾"

3"

3½"

2"

1½"

1½"

1½"

1¼"

1½"

¾"

¾"

⅜" DIA

BASE BLOCK ¾" x 2" x 5½"

Pickup with removable camper invites addition of boat and trailer; modify semi-trailer plans to suit.

PICKUP TRUCK

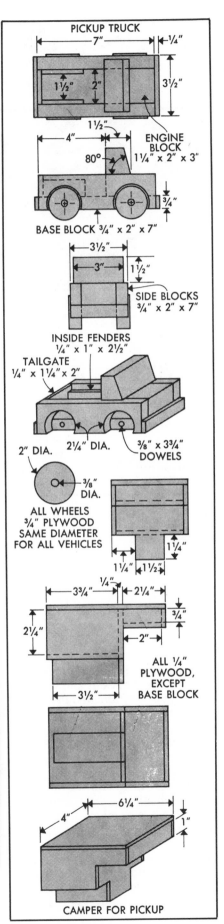

7"

¼"

1½"

2"

3½"

1½"

ENGINE BLOCK 1¼" x 2" x 3"

4"

80°

¾"

BASE BLOCK ¾" x 2" x 7"

3½"

3"

1½"

SIDE BLOCKS ¾" x 2" x 7"

INSIDE FENDERS ¼" x 1" x 2½"

TAILGATE ¼" x 1¼" x 2"

2" DIA.

2¼" DIA.

⅜" x 3¾" DOWELS

⅜" DIA.

ALL WHEELS ¾" PLYWOOD SAME DIAMETER FOR ALL VEHICLES

1¼"

1¼"

1½"

¼"

3¾"

2¼"

¾"

2¼"

2"

3½"

ALL ¼" PLYWOOD, EXCEPT BASE BLOCK

6¼"

4"

1"

CAMPER FOR PICKUP

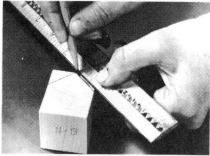

Mark roof angles on end of building as indicated in diagram, showing side view of individual building.

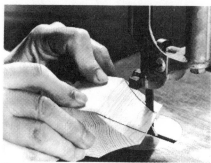

For two-angle roofs, cut first set, then mark and cut second. Hold flat surface down firmly as you feed into blade.

Sand all surfaces thoroughly, then glue together parts of buildings made from more than one block.

Village Blocks

To a small child this little story-book village is a fascinating source for hours of imaginative play. The buildings were inspired by old fashioned European wooden toys that used to fill Christmas stockings.

Use pine blocks of three thicknesses, 3/4 in., 1-1/8 in. and 1-1/2 in., to make the buildings. Be sure you make no buildings small enough for a child to put in his mouth and choke on. This is no toy for tiny tots who will view the buildings as chewables. Cut blocks to size from the proper thickness for each building, then shape roofs to fit. Some buildings are shaped from single blocks, some built up.

Cut the blocks to the dimensions given in the diagrams and mark the roof angles as indicated in the side view of each building. Saw roof to shape. In some instances, a roof may have two sets of angles; after sawing the first set, mark the second one. Hold the building firmly on the saw table and feed the peak into the blade.

Sand all surfaces smooth, then glue together the parts of those buildings made from more than one block. Use any good non-toxic finish to paint the surfaces a solid color or to antique them so they will resemble their original European counterparts.

When the paint dries, put on windows and doors with an indelible marking pen. If you desire a "lighted" window effect, *before painting the buildings* paint yellow areas on the buildings where the windows will be located. Mark the window areas lightly in pencil, paint around them with the building color, then mark the window details with pen.

Add people and trees lathe-turned from birch or maple to complete the village. Several designs for these final touches are given.

You'll add to everyone's pleasure with the project if you make a large "village hall" toy box for storage. Scale up the design for House K, use 3/4 in. plywood for the shell, hinge the roof and attach a handle.

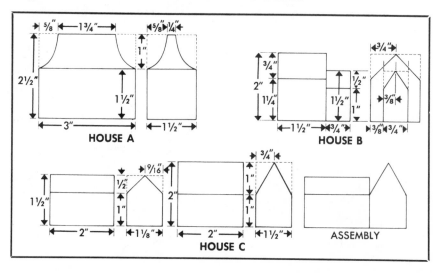

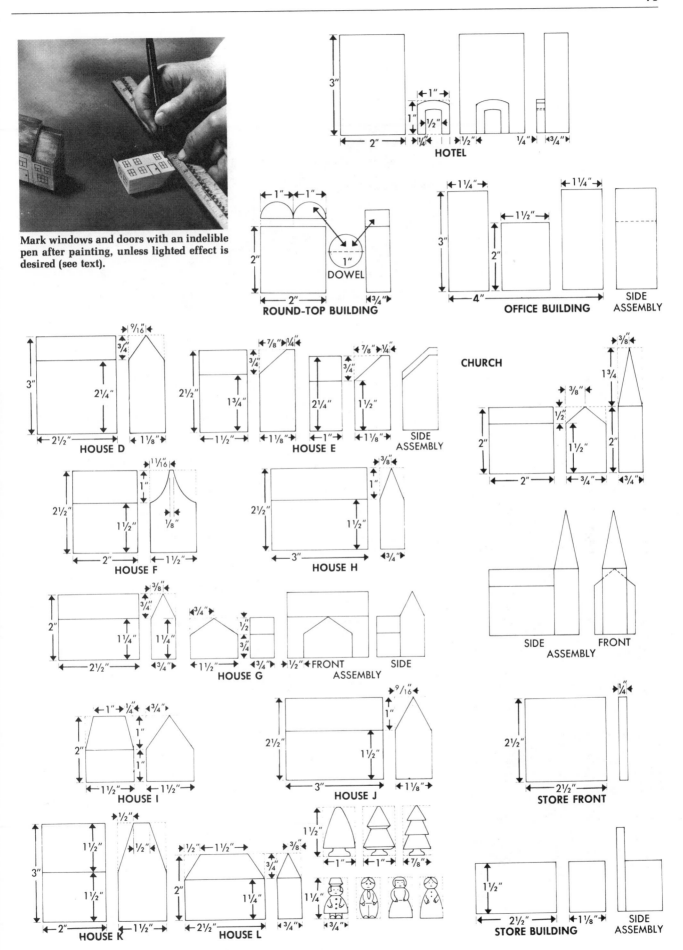

Mark windows and doors with an indelible pen after painting, unless lighted effect is desired (see text).

HOTEL

ROUND-TOP BUILDING

DOWEL

OFFICE BUILDING

SIDE ASSEMBLY

HOUSE D

HOUSE E

SIDE ASSEMBLY

CHURCH

SIDE ASSEMBLY

FRONT

HOUSE F

HOUSE H

HOUSE G

FRONT

ASSEMBLY

SIDE

SIDE

ASSEMBLY

FRONT

HOUSE I

HOUSE J

STORE FRONT

HOUSE K

HOUSE L

STORE BUILDING

SIDE ASSEMBLY

Building Blocks

Building blocks are as old as toys, as young as tomorrow. Make them from scrap wood, give your youngsters years of constructive fun.

Generations of American children have had hours of fun building log houses, forts and even modern skyscrapers with these simple blocks. Here's a genuine "fun" toy that fosters creativity in children.

Oak was used in the original blocks; this tough material lasts longer than most woods, but maple or other close-grained hardwood can be substituted. Start by ripping the stock into 1/4 x 1-3/4 in. strips. Cut the blocks to length before cutting the notches. A dado blade set at 5/16 in. will simplify cutting the notches.

A hole is drilled in the top piece for a flag pole. The flag is the type used on a bicycle and can be obtained at many hardware and novelty stores.

Hone off all the sharp edges on the blocks with sandpaper, then stain them, over which nontoxic varnish is applied. You also can enamel the blocks in various colors if a particular child is more intrigued by bright colors, and more attracted to the modern than pioneer buildings.

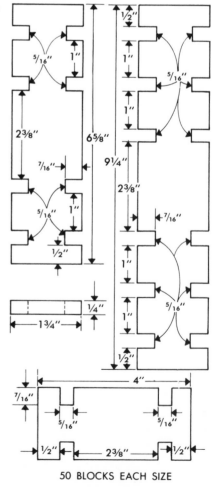

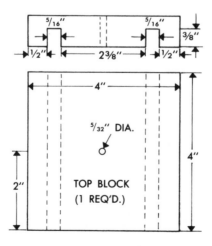

TOP BLOCK (1 REQ'D.)

50 BLOCKS EACH SIZE

Gravity Marble Game

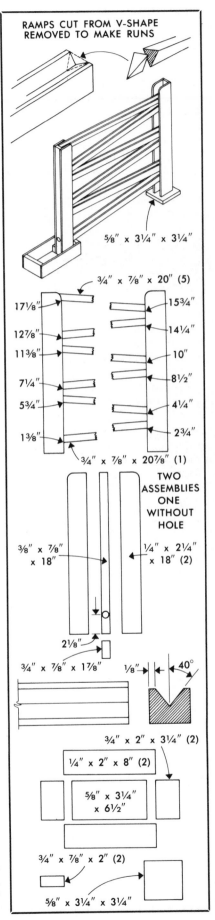

RAMPS CUT FROM V-SHAPE
REMOVED TO MAKE RUNS

5/8" x 3¼" x 3¼"

¾" x ⅞" x 20" (5)

17⅛"   15¾"
12⅞"   14¼"
11⅜"   10"
7¼"   8½"
5¾"   4¼"
1⅜"   2¾"

¾" x ⅞" x 20⅞" (1)

TWO
ASSEMBLIES
ONE
WITHOUT
HOLE

⅜" x ⅞" x 18"   ¼" x 2¼" x 18" (2)

2⅛"

¾" x ⅞" x 1⅞"   ⅛"   40°

¾" x 2" x 3¼" (2)

¼" x 2" x 8" (2)

⅝" x 3¼" x 6½"

¾" x ⅞" x 2" (2)

⅝" x 3¼" x 3¼"

This simple game that consists of marbles rolling down slanting ramps continues to fascinate both young and old.

Construction is quite easy, with the only challenge being the cutting of the V-channels in the marble runs. On a table saw, set the blade at 40 degrees and lower it until it projects just 5/8 in. above the table. Move the rip fence over to 1/8 in. from the blade.

Using a push stick and a hold-down stick for added safety, run the 3/4 x 7/8 in. strips over the saw in one direction, then reverse each strip and run it back in the other direction. A V-shape strip should fall loose.

Assemble the end "towers" from the designated strips and bore a hole near the bottom of one to allow the marbles to exit into the box.

Use the scrap V-shape pieces to make small "ramps" to insert in the upper end of each run. They speed up the marbles and prevent a row of marbles from dropping on each other.

To make the ramps, cut a 45 degree angle about 1/2 in. from the end of the V-strip, then saw at right angles about 1/2 in. from the angle cut. You will need five of the ramps, which are glued and held with a single countersunk brad in the high end of each run.

Build the box in which the marbles collect, then glue in the two small blocks that position the bottom of the tower and also prevent the marbles from rolling into the small areas beside the bottom of the tower.

Fit one tower with a base 3-1/4 in. square. Mark on each tower the locations of the runs, then glue and brad the runs to the insides of the towers. Note that the high end of each run fits to the back of the towers, while the low ends are spaced to allow the marbles to drop between the ends of the runs and the backs of the towers.

Finish the game with bright colors for little youngsters, a stain and varnish being more practical for older children.

Bulldozer

Bulldozers hold a great fascination for almost everyone, as can be seen at a building site where one is being operated.

It thunders, snorts and roars, under the control of one man, as it goes about its job of piling up huge mounds of dirt or pushing over buildings or trees. Manufactured toy copies of the mechanical monster too often have tracks that come off, blades that break off and pieces and parts that simply won't stay in place.

This wooden version of the machine has no tracks to lose and its blade is a heavy assembly that will move as much sand or dirt as the childpower engine can handle.

Check the drawing carefully and you'll see that most of the components of the 'dozer can be cut and shaped from scraps of wood. Softwood is fine, but hardwood will add to the wearing quality of the "tracks" and the blade which get the most wear and tear.

Two recesses are indicated on the inside surface of each track. Wooden wheels are turned to 2-1/2 in. diameter. You might have wheels of a slightly different size, and if so, make the recesses to accommodate them. Just be sure the wheels project below the tracks enough to assure easy rolling on a bumpy surface. Allow at least 1/4 in. to 1/2 in. clearance.

No provision was made on the blade for it to be held up, nor for any rolling assist. You might want to use a somewhat larger diameter screw in each blade arm, and snug it up so the blade stays where it's positioned.

A couple of small rollers recessed into the bottom edge of the blade would assure easy rolling on a floor, without limiting the effectiveness of the blade when used outdoors to push dirt or sand.

Use a waterproof glue and brass screws if the toy is to be used outdoors. The model shown is unfinished, but real bulldozers generally are painted a bright yellow, with moving parts such as the blade arms painted with diagonal black

stripes as a safety measure. The back of the rig also has the diagonal black stripes.

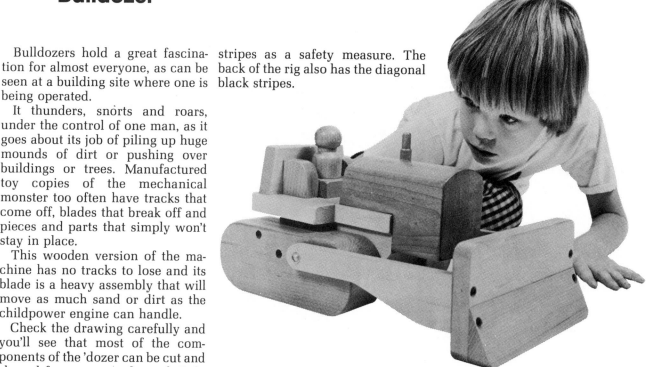

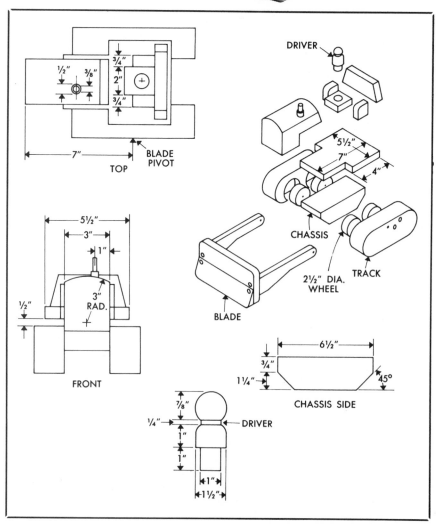

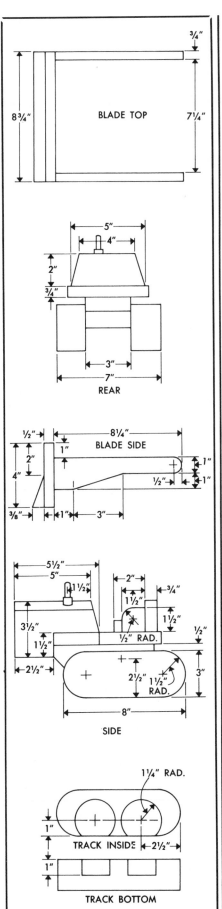

Dump Truck

Pieces of 1 and 2 in. stock from the scrap box are used to make this action toy in just an hour or two.

Cut the "chassis" from a piece of 1 x 4 and notch the end as shown. Drill a 3/8 in. hole through the chassis across the notch.

The "hood" of the truck is a piece of 2 x 4 with the front edge beveled as indicated then glued and nailed to the chassis. Slice two 1/4 in. sections from a 1/2 in. dowel to make headlights that are glued and bradded to the front.

The "cab" is a block of wood notched as shown. This can be done on a table or radial arm saw with a dado blade, or you can use a handsaw to make four cuts, then chisel out the waste between the four posts. The top of the cab is beveled on the front edge, and glued and bradded to the posts.

The dump body is made of 1/2 or 3/4 in. stock—whatever is in the scrap box—to the dimensions given. A small piece of 1 in. scrap (3/4 in. net) is cut to make the "tilt block" that is drilled for the 3/8 in. dowel that fits through the notch in the chassis. The "tail gate" of the truck is held only by two screws at the top that let it swing open when the truck body is tilted, so the cargo is dumped.

Wheels are cut or turned from 1 and 2 in. stock. Use a fly cutter in a drill press, or a hole saw in a portable electric drill.

Paint the finished truck with lead-free enamels in bright colors.

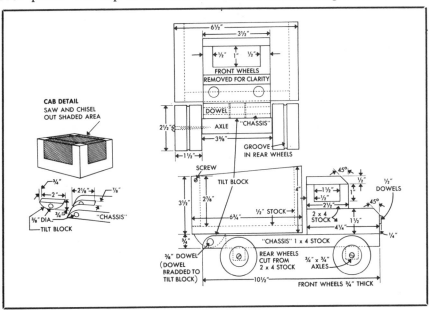

Complete the job by applying the decorative stripe around the entire vehicle.

Ready for show or go, this vehicle will transport favorite dolls in style; all it needs is a CB, stereo and waterbed.

Motor Home

Little boys especially will be thrilled to play with this scaled down version of a motor home.

Use solid-core birch plywood for most of the construction. This material has a good dense surface that accepts paint very well. Whatever material you choose should have a comparable surface.

Start work by cutting the sides to size. Lay out the perimeters of the door and window openings and cut them. For clean, splinter-free cuts, tape over all marked lines first and keep the good side of the plywood up. Cut wheel-well openings in the sides and clean up all edges.

The floor should be cut next. Make certain that the stair opening in the floor will coincide with the door opening on the passenger side.

Next, cut and shape the front and back top spacers, following the profiles given in the squared drawings. Use pine for these components.

Assemble the body shell, less the top, as follows: glue and nail the sides to the floor, glue and clamp the spacers between the sides at the top ends, then add the front and back panels. Set all nails and fill holes with a wood filler.

Cut and trim the top so that it fits loosely between the sides and is supported firmly across its entire width by the rabbets in the spacers. Make a series of shallow parallel cuts in the top to simulate ribbing.

Cut and fit the wheel retainers, window and door trim. The retainers are mounted inside the sides and flush with the side-bottom edges, where they are glued and clamped. Glue and brad the window and door trim in place.

To complete the main assembly, cut and fit the interior room dividers and attach them with glue and brads. Set the assembly aside, cut and fit (but do not attach) all remaining components, then sand all pieces and paint as desired. Preferably use good, hard enamels for the body and trim, and wait to apply the decorative "wraparound" stripe until all other remaining steps have been completed.

When you're done with the painting, attach the stairs with glue and nails. Fit and mount the door after the stairs have been fastened in place.

Use contact adhesive to apply indoor-outdoor carpet scraps or some other material to the floor, then mount all other interior and exterior pieces as shown. Note that 1 in. diameter hardwood drawer pulls are used to simulate forward roof vents and 1 in. diameter steel furniture glides for headlights.

Also note the wheel mounting technique. The wheels are mounted on No. 10 x 2 in. roundhead screws, with 1/4 in. washers between the wheels and screw heads and wheels and body. The washers serve as friction bearings.

Interior has adequate space for furnishings built to suit; indoor-outdoor carpet is secured with contact adhesive.

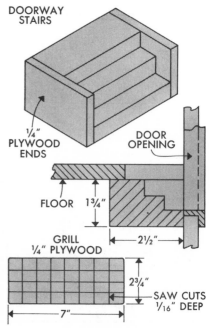

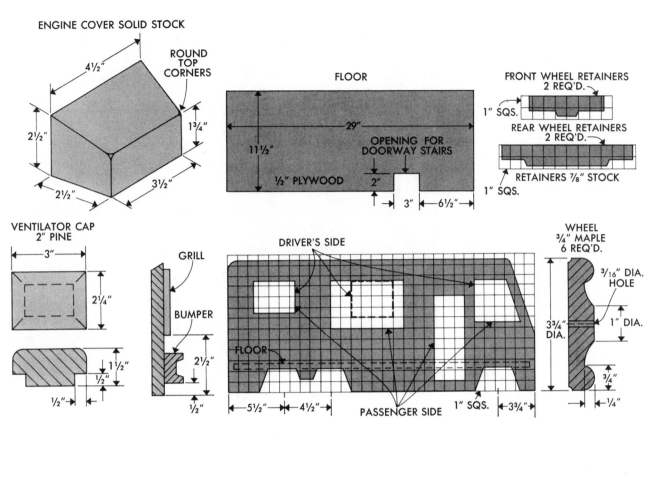

ENGINE COVER SOLID STOCK

ROUND TOP CORNERS

4½"

2½"

1¾"

3½"

2½"

FLOOR

29"

11½"

½" PLYWOOD

OPENING FOR DOORWAY STAIRS

2"

3"

6½"

FRONT WHEEL RETAINERS
2 REQ'D.

1" SQS.

REAR WHEEL RETAINERS
2 REQ'D.

RETAINERS ⅞" STOCK

1" SQS.

VENTILATOR CAP
2" PINE

3"

2¼"

1½"

½"

½"

GRILL

BUMPER

2½"

½"

DRIVER'S SIDE

FLOOR

5½"

4½"

PASSENGER SIDE

1" SQS.

3¾"

WHEEL
¾" MAPLE
6 REQ'D.

3/16" DIA. HOLE

1" DIA.

3¾" DIA.

¾"

¼"

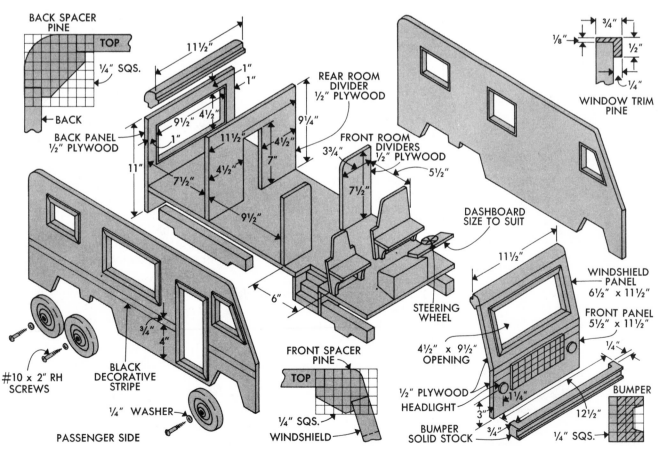

BACK SPACER PINE

TOP

¼" SQS.

BACK

BACK PANEL
½" PLYWOOD

11½"

1"

1"

9½"

4½"

1"

11½"

4½"

7"

4½"

11"

7½"

9½"

REAR ROOM DIVIDER
½" PLYWOOD

9¼"

FRONT ROOM DIVIDERS
½" PLYWOOD

3¾"

7½"

5½"

DASHBOARD SIZE TO SUIT

STEERING WHEEL

6"

FRONT SPACER PINE

TOP

¼" SQS.

WINDSHIELD

¾"

½"

1/8"

¼"

WINDOW TRIM PINE

11½"

WINDSHIELD PANEL
6½" x 11½"

FRONT PANEL
5½" x 11½"

¼"

4½" x 9½" OPENING

½" PLYWOOD
HEADLIGHT

1¼"

3"

BUMPER SOLID STOCK

¾"

12½"

¼" SQS.

BUMPER

¾"
4"

BLACK DECORATIVE STRIPE

#10 x 2" RH SCREWS

¼" WASHER

PASSENGER SIDE

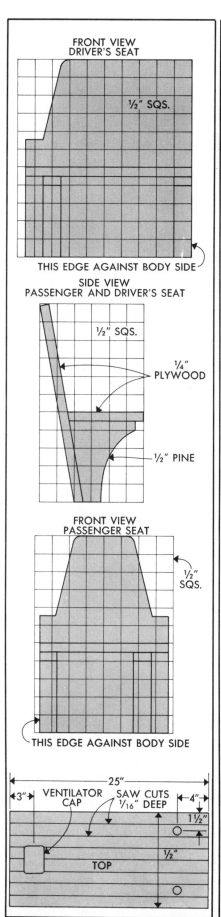

FRONT VIEW
DRIVER'S SEAT

½" SQS.

THIS EDGE AGAINST BODY SIDE

SIDE VIEW
PASSENGER AND DRIVER'S SEAT

½" SQS.

¼"
PLYWOOD

½" PINE

FRONT VIEW
PASSENGER SEAT

½"
SQS.

THIS EDGE AGAINST BODY SIDE

25"

3"   VENTILATOR   SAW CUTS   4"
CAP   1/16" DEEP

1½"

TOP   ½"

Tug and Barge

Children enjoy simple toys they can push around on the floor, and over which they have complete control. Boats have a particular fascination. This tug and barge set will provide years of fun for youngsters.

If softwood is used for the set, 1-1/2 in. stair lumber is ideal. Hardwood is a better bet for appearance and resistance to the battering the toys will get if used outdoors. Maple or birch are excellent for the purpose.

For the tug, cut a paper template and use it to mark out the hull shape on a block 1-1/2 x 5-1/2 x 11-1/2 in. Lightly pencil in a center line from bow to stern to aid in positioning the above-deck structures later.

Saw out the hull, then sand the sides smooth. The rounded front of the bridge roof can be cut next.

Now, cut the cabin and bridge sections from 1-1/2 x 2-1/2 in. stock. Be sure to cut both ends of the bridge, and one end of the cabin, at a 10 degree angle. Check the two pieces to make sure the angles are exact and that they mate properly. That is, that the front of the cabin and the back of the bridge meet in a tight joint. Sand a bit if necessary to create a neat fit.

Bore the hole in the cabin 1 in. diameter and 3/4 in. deep to accept the stack. Note that this also is raked back at a 10 degree angle. Cut the stack from a piece of 1 in. dowel, making it about 3-7/8 in. long. Sand the top at an angle to be parallel to the deck, which will bring it down to a height approximately 3 in. above the top of the cabin.

Sand all parts smooth, then use glue and nails to assemble. Countersunk screws will create a stronger assembly.

You may want to make several barges so they can be hooked up in a "barge train."

Note that this is an "ocean-going" tug, rather than a river tug. The latter have blunt bows and they push a "tow" of barges rather than pulling them as do ocean tugs.

Each rectangular barge has a 10 degree angle at bow and stern. Bore the 3/8 in. holes 3/4 in. deep near each corner. Sand all surfaces and round off all sharp edges. Glue the dowel bridle posts in the holes and, when the glue has set, round off the tops of the posts with sandpaper.

If a toddler is to use the tug and barge, shorten the stack on the tug and round the top. Also shorten the bridle posts on the barge so they project only about 1 in., and sand the tops round and smooth.

Drive a screw eye into the stern of the tug and attach a tow line such as nylon cord. Make a loop in the end of the cord so it can be dropped over the bridle post on the barge.

If several barges are to be "towed," make a line for each pair of barges, with loops at both ends of the line.

Paint the tug and the barge in bright colors with nontoxic, lead-free enamel. Most such paints will have a "child-safe" listing on the label.

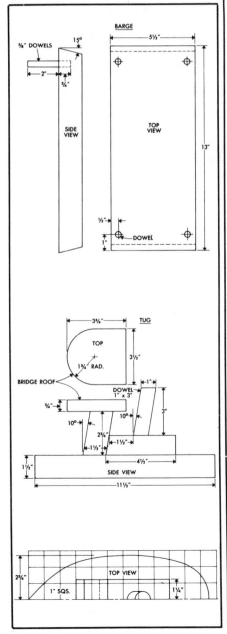

Biplane

Your little aviator will be scanning the skies for a chance to take on the Red Baron or imitate the aerobatics of a barnstorming daredevil if you build this sturdy little airplane. Reminiscent of the Spad or Sopwith Camel of World War I, this rugged biplane is designed to stand up to the roughest of pilots and the worst of landing fields.

Its constantly spinning plexiglass propeller is not easy to break, yet it presents no hazard.

All parts of the plane can be easily shaped with hand tools, except the cowling at the front, which requires some whittling, filing and sanding. A lathe would permit shaping the cowling in a matter of minutes.

You can make patterns for the component parts by enlarging the squared drawings.

The cross section of the fuselage behind the cowling is an octagon with the corner surfaces a bit shorter than the top, bottom and sides. After shaping the octagon the full length of a stick 2 in. square and 8 in. long, the sides are angled back to create a 1 in. width at the back end of the fuselage. A notch is cut for the bottom wing and slots for the tail assembly.

The cowling is attached to the forward end of the fuselage with glue and two screws driven into the two counterbored holes in the cowling.

The rugged landing gear is a block shaped as indicated, to which the 1/2 x 1 in. diameter wheels are attached. The bottom wing is attached next, then the landing gear is fastened to it.

The strut for the top wing is cut to shape and glued and screwed to the fuselage, then the top wing is attached.

Shape the rudder and elevators and attach them to the fuselage. A "whirling propeller," actually a 1/4 x 4 in. circle of clear plexiglass with edges sanded round and smooth, is center-bored and screwed to the nose of the plane. Finally paint the plane as a World War I replica or perhaps with a brighter color of an air show daredevil's plane.

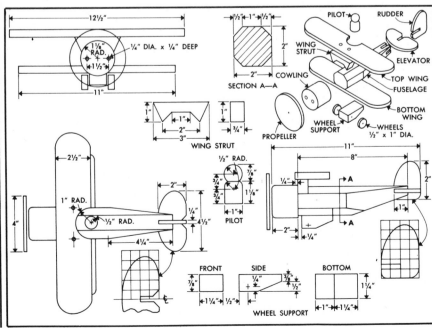

Helicopter

While this toy helicopter is as modern as today, its construction is as basic as toy building blocks, and you can create a dozen if a fleet of the "choppers" is needed to outfit the neighborhood youngsters.

A hardwood or softwood 4 x 4 is the stock used. Start by cutting off the four corners of a 10 in. length of 4 x 4 (or several pieces of 1 in. stock glued up to make a block) to 45 degrees x 1 in. A bit more or less than 1 in. will cause no problems.

Mark the back from the front end of the block 4-3/4 in. and cut a 45 degree notch at the top and bottom of the block. The top then is cut straight back to the tail end of the fuselage, while the bottom is cut at an angle to create a length of 3/4 in. at the end, as shown on the drawing.

The sides are cut at an angle, equally, to produce a width of 1 in. at the tail end of the fuselage. The nose of the fuselage now is cut and sanded as indicated to create the streamlined shape.

Drill the four holes in the lower angles of the fuselage for the struts that support the floats, centering them on the angled surface.

The floats are lengths of 1 in. dowel with the ends rounded. Drill 1/4 in. blind holes in the floats the same spacing as on the fuselage, then glue the struts and floats to the fuselage.

The supports for the main and tail rotors are shaped as indicated. They can be simple lathe turnings made on a screw center or, lacking a lathe, they can be carved by hand. You might want to make the supports a tear-drop shape front to back, rather than having them round as shown.

The main and tail rotors are cut from clear 3/8 in. sheet plastic with edges rounded and smoothed. For a touch of color you might want to use a plastic that is red or blue or some bright hue. The original helicopter was finished with clear varnish, but you might want to paint yours.

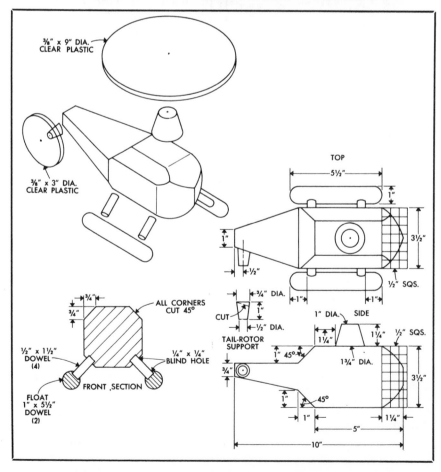

Antique "Dolly Madison" Coupe

Children of all ages will love this novel toy, and when well made it will last several generations. Only hand tools are required, although power tools will permit "mass-production" of the coupe if you wish to make a number for gifts.

Pine or other straight grained softwood is best. Cut all the pieces to size and shape, then start assembly by gluing together the three pieces (3) that form the trunk. Next, glue the dash panel (4) to the hood and radiator (1, 2) and the seat back (5) to the trunk. Glue the seat blocks together (6, 7) and to the seat back. Install the steering wheel post and steering wheel. Glue trunk and seat assembly to the chassis (8), then attach the doors with glue-soaked strips of denim, fitting

pieces of waxed paper or aluminum foil between the folds to prevent their adhering together. When the glue is dry, pivot the doors to loosen the hinges, then assemble the rest of the car.

The finished car is sanded and all edges rounded. Apply antiquing or paint with bright colored, nontoxic enamels.

Materials List

All 1" pine (3/4" net)
1. 2-1/4" x 2-1/4" (2)
1A. 3/4" x 3/4" (2)
2. 2-1/4" x 2-1/4" (1)
3. 2-1/4" x 2-1/4" (3)
4. 2-1/4" x 2-7/8" (1
5. 2-1/4" x 6" (1)
6. 1" x 2-1/4" (1)
7. 7/8" x 2-1/4" (1)
8. 2-1/4" x 9-3/4" (1)
9. 1-3/4" x 2-7/8" (2)
10. 3-3/4" x 4-1/2" (1)
11. 1/2" x 2-7/8" (2)
12. 3/4" x 3" (2)
13. 3/4" x 2-1/2" (2)
14. 1/2" x 2-1/2" (2)
15. 1-3/8" x 8-3/4" (2)
16. 3/4" x 8-3/4" (2)
17. 1/8" x 1/2" x 2-5/8" (1)
18. 2-7/8" dia. disk (5)
   Hardwood Dowels
19. 1/2" x 5" (2)
20. 3/4" x 1" dia. (4)
21. 1/2" dia. x 1" (2)
22. 5/8" x 1" dia. (2)
23. 1/2" dia. x 1" (1)
24. 1/4" x 1" dia. (1)
25. 1/2" dia. x 1" (1)
26. 1" dia. x 1-1/8" (2)
27. 1/2" dia. x 1/4" (2)
28. 1/2" dia. x 1/2" (1)
29. 1/4" dia. x 1/4" (30—6 each wheel)

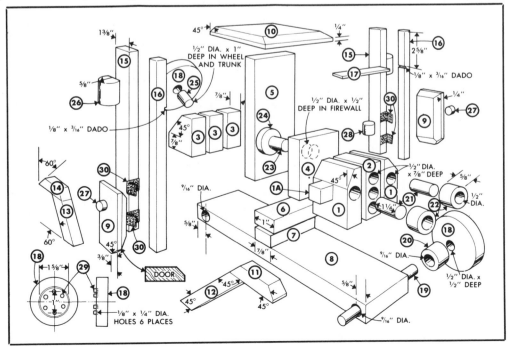

Junior Steam Train

Steam locomotives are described by the number of large drive wheels and the smaller, auxiliary wheels. For example, a big long haul engine might be an "eight-four-two" which means eight drivers and six smaller wheels, either ahead of or behind the drivers.

This yard engine has six drive wheels, and no auxiliaries, hence it's called a "Six-Oh." The resulting short wheelbase allows the engine to run on short-radius turns, as in a railroad yard.

The car it pulls through the switching yard can be of any type, but we've shown a tank car, box car, gondola or hopper and the ever-present caboose. There is no coal tender behind the engine because it's not a "play car" to a child, but you might add one of your own design.

Scraps of any kind of wood can be used to make the various cars and the engine. A lathe will permit turning the boiler of the engine and the tank for the car, but they can be whittled, filed and sanded to shape with hand tools.

Wheels are 1-1/8 in. in diameter, but 1/2 in. slices of 1 or 1-1/4 in. dowel would do quite nicely.

The two domes, the stack and the whistle on the engine can be shaped by carving, or you might assemble them from pieces of dowel. The stack has a tapered shape, but you can use a piece of straight dowel with some loss of authenticity in appearance.

Stack all the engine wheels and drill screw holes for the connector bar, and drill both bars at the same time. This will assure accurate alignment of the various parts so they will operate smoothly in unison. Use washers under the heads of the roundhead wood screws that connect the bars to the wheels, so there is easy action.

Cut the various pieces of the engine to size and shape and join them with glue and screws from underneath where possible. Brads can be used to attach the roof of the engine cab. Countersink them and cover the heads with wood putty.

The chassis of all the cars is the same size, 3-1/2 x 9 in., cut from 1 in. stock, 3/4 in. net. The tank is flattened slightly on the bottom and attached with glue and screws. The dome at the top is a length of 1-1/2 in. dowel shaped and fitted in a hole in the tank. A piece of 1/2 in. stock 2-1/4 in. square is center bored and fitted down over the dome.

The hopper/gondola has the "dumpers" fastened to the bottom of the chassis, then the sides are attached vertically to the top, and the ends are glued and bradded inside the angled ends of the sides.

The caboose is assembled from a series of blocks, glued and bradded.

The box car has sliding doors that slide in grooves chiseled in the chassis and roof. The top and bottom of the doors are rabbeted as shown to create the projections that fit in the grooves.

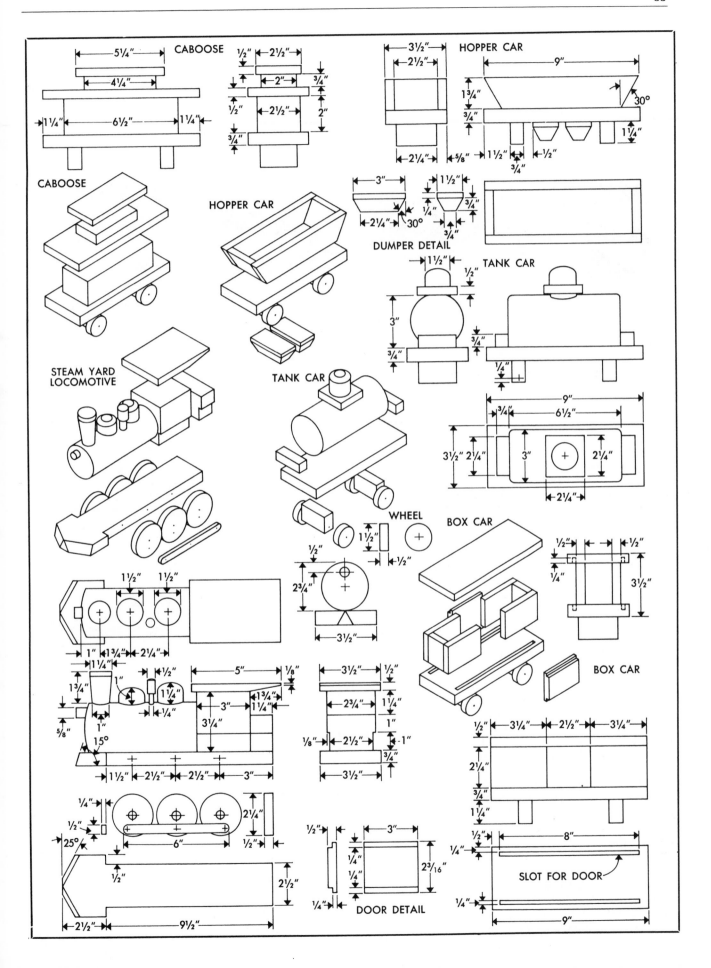

Ride'em Steam Train

Young engineers will be delighted with this train that is rugged enough to carry a passenger. Two of the units, the caboose and gondola car, can be used to haul a child's cargo, or be used as small toy boxes.

Almost any kind of wood can be used. The train is a joy to make, and everyone will marvel at the ease with which it moves and the way each piece of rolling stock follows the other because of the swiveling front trucks.

All four pieces have similarities, to simplify building. Starting with the engine, cut the sides, front, back and top of the cab. Make the cutouts, rabbets and dadoes as required. Before assembing, give all pieces a coat of sealer and paint the insides black. The hardwood axle for the larger back wheels is turned from hardwood and fits in holes bored in the cab sides. A whittled dowel may be substituted. The large wheels have 3/4 in. holes in them so they turn on the axle.

The four smaller front wheels of the engine are the same thickness and diameter as those for the remaining cars, and 28 of them are required for the complete train.

The engine boiler may be turned in a lathe from a splined and glued "billet" assembled from clear, straight-grained stock. It can be a bit under or over the 7 in. diameter shown. The boiler can be hand hewn with the aid of a drawknife or plane. A hole is bored to accept the smokestack, and the bottom is flattened slightly so it sits flat on the floor of the assembly.

Axles for the front wheels of the engine are the same as for all the rolling stock, but here, as for the back wheels on the rolling stock, the axle assemblies are attached solidly to the basic floor.

Start the engine assembly by nailing on the back of the cab, then the two sides and the front. Set all nails, cover with wood putty and sand smooth when it is dry. Attach the top last, nailing, filling and sanding.

Attach the two front axles with No. 10 x 2 in. flathead screws. Attach the boiler with two screws, then tap the smokestack into the hole, adding a touch of glue. When the large wheels are installed, with their restraining wheel caps, the engine is complete.

The gondola is the easiest of the four pieces to make as it is just the

Engine has "truck" at front end with four small wheels, two larger ones under the cab itself.

basic floor to which four sides are joined. Trim strips are applied with glue and 1/2 in. brads. The back axles are attached solidly to the floor, while the front "truck" swivels on a 1/4 in. carriage bolt. A double nut locks the truck.

This method of attaching the truck is utilized on all the other cars as well. As on the engine, wheel caps secure the wheels to the axles.

The tank car has the same basic floor as the other cars, and the fixed axles are at the back, with the swiveling truck at the front. The tank is made in the same manner as the boiler of the engine.

Tank ends are fashioned from 2 in. pine and made to the same diameter as the tank. A small bevel is cut on the ends of the tank proper, and the two ends, so a V-shape groove is created when the ends are joined to the tank.

Three saddles of 1 in. softwood are cut to the shape indicated. Make the curve to suit your tank, as it may be a bit larger or smaller than the 7 in. suggested for the tank.

Space the saddles on the floor of the car as dimensioned, and fasten them with glue and No. 8 x 2 in. flathead screws, using two for each saddle.

It is easier to enamel all the pieces before assembly. All clearance holes for the screws are drilled first and the car is dry-assembled, then taken apart for painting.

Three colors are used on the tank car: the tank itself is aluminum, the saddles a dark gray and the remainder of the car black. The wheels rotate on well-waxed axles and are held on securely by wheel caps.

Each car has fixed rear truck with four wheels, while front truck pivots on bolt. Note screweyes in trucks.

Cylinder of tank car is painted silver, the saddles are dark gray, while the rest of the car is black.

Underside of engine shows how axle for big wheels goes through sides of the cab. Note rabbets.

Every train has a caboose and this one not only is a caboose, but it also serves as a miniature toy box. Construction is simple; the caboose is simply a box with a swing-up lid. The lid is the roof of the caboose plus the cupola and its roof.

To keep weight down, the cupola is assembled from four walls and a one-piece roof.

The roof of the caboose has a

When the roof is lifted on the caboose it turns out to be a miniature toy box. Use small butt hinges, light chain.

Caboose is painted bright orange, with black wheels, roofs and platforms. Orange also is used inside caboose.

framework to support the two pieces of 1/4 in. plywood or solid stock.

The wheels, floor, roofs and platforms are black; the rest is bright orange, including the inside.

Because it is a pull train, you'll need a stout cord on the engine, at the end of which you can make a loop or attach a length of dowel for a handle.

Between the cars you'll need tow bars, assembled from two "clamps" and a length of dowel. Make the tow bars of hardwood, as they must endure considerable stress and strain.

Screweyes are driven into the front end of each swiveling truck, into the back axle of each car and the back axle of the engine. The ends of the tow bars are fitted over the screweyes, then a 1/4 x 1-1/4 in. carriage bolt and nut is used at each coupling to join the train together.

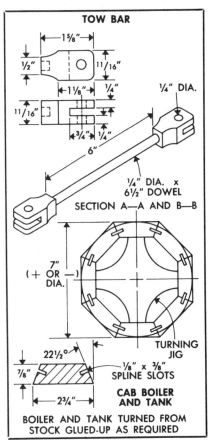

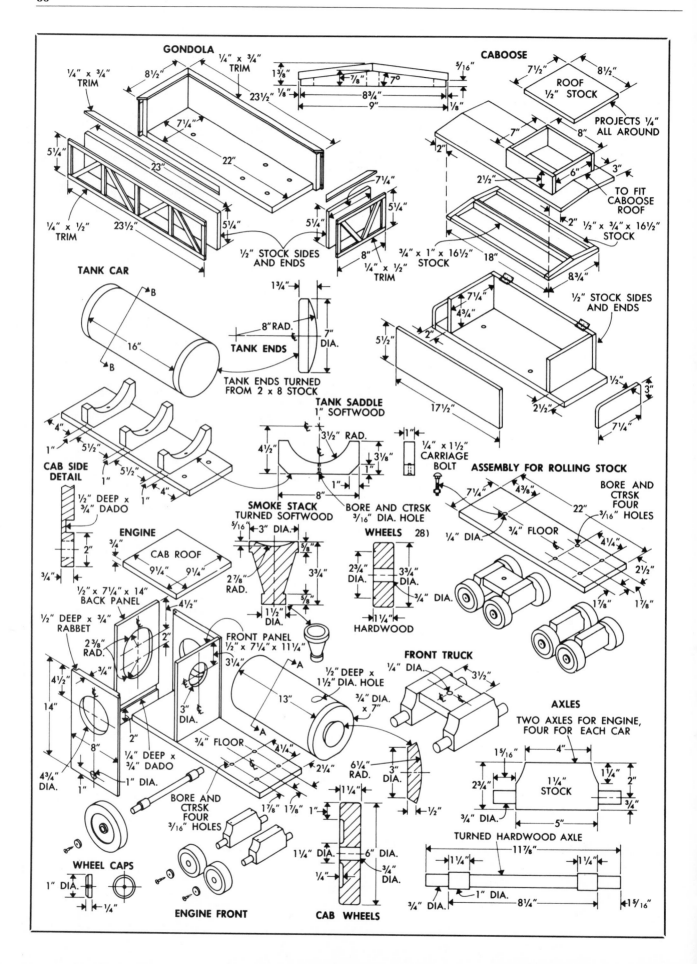

Ride'em Riverboat

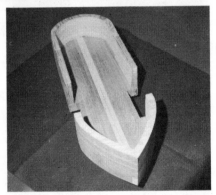

Hull is built up with U-shapes for stern, V-shapes for bow cut from 3/4 in. plywood as indicated.

Cabin is assembled in much the same manner as the hull, with built-up U-shapes at each end cut from solid stock.

Rubber-tired wheels are on axles made from 1/2 x 3-1/2 in. cap screws. Wood screws are driven through axles.

A youngster can pretend to be a real riverboat captain with this side-wheeler under his command. It "floats" on two rubber-tired wheels near the front and a rubber-wheeled caster at the stern so no marks are left on the floor.

A stem caster was used for the original but a plate type could be used instead. Be sure the caster is a size that, combined with the wheels, keeps the boat on an even keel.

The hull and cabin get their depth and shape from glued together sections cut from plywood or solid stock as indicated. The hull has a top and bottom, while the cabin has neither. It sits on the hull and the top deck rests on it.

Attach the top and bottom of the hull with glue and screws, after first gluing and screwing the cabin to the top of the hull.

The top deck is machined as detailed in the drawing, then glued and screwed to the top of the cabin.

Note also that two holes in the underside of the top deck near the front, and one at the back, accept dowels that are support columns between the top deck and the top of the hull.

The width and length of the notches in the bottom of the hull may vary a bit from the dimensions shown, depending on the size of the wheels selected.

The wheelboxes are cut from 1/2 in. plywood and glued and nailed to the sides of the hull. While the wheelhouse on the original is a turning, it can be a rectangle with rounded corners, if you don't have a lathe. A roof should be added, and it overhangs all around. Windows are painted on the front, with a center divider at the very front.

Paint the cabin and the cabin windows before you do the assembly. Any minor flaws that occur during assembly can later be touched up with paint.

The twin smokestacks and the brace between should be solidly glued to the top deck. Bore the 1 in. holes for the stacks all the way through the 3/4 in. thickness of the top deck, so the bottom ends of the stacks rest on the tops of the cabin walls. The reason for the need for strength in the stack assembly is that it is the "handle" by which the young captain will control his craft.

Paint the finished boat in bright colors, then tack a length of rope around the hull near the "waterline" just below the top of the hull. This is the "bumper" to avoid damaging anything with which the riverboat accidentally comes in contact.

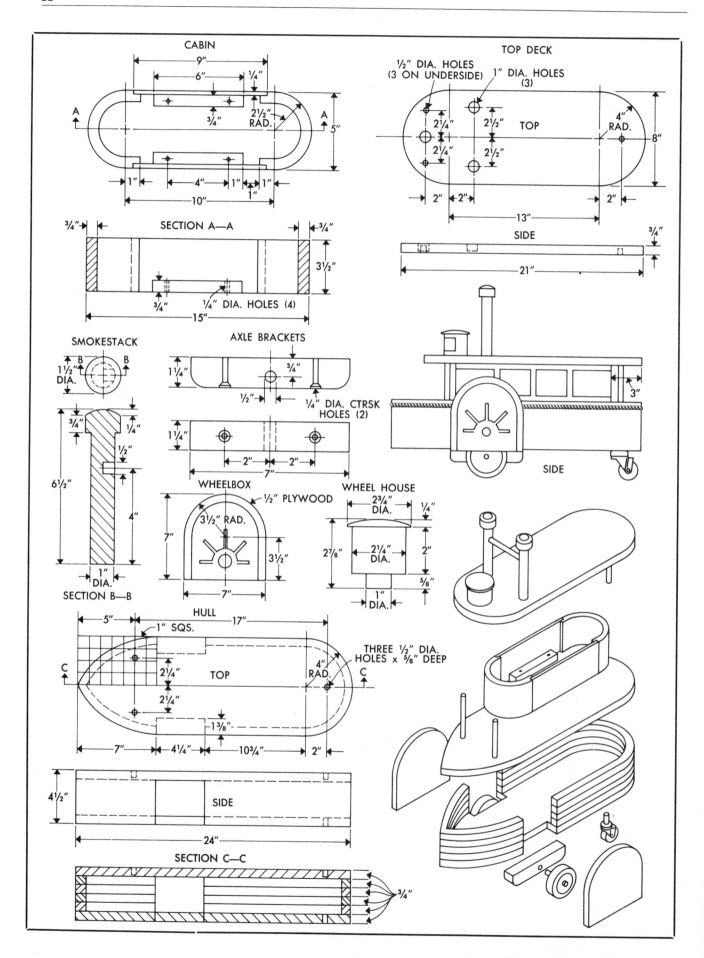

CABIN

9"
6"
¼"
¾"
2½" RAD.
A   A
5"
1"
4"
1"
1"
1"
10"

SECTION A—A
¾"   ¾"
3½"
¾"
¼" DIA. HOLES (4)
15"

SMOKESTACK
B   B
1½" DIA.
¾"
¼"
½"
6½"
4"
1" DIA.
SECTION B—B

AXLE BRACKETS
1¼"
¾"
½"
¼" DIA. CTRSK HOLES (2)
1¼"
2"   2"
7"

WHEELBOX
½" PLYWOOD
3½" RAD.
7"
3½"
7"

WHEEL HOUSE
2¾" DIA.
¼"
2⅞"
2¼" DIA.
2"
⅝"
1" DIA.

HULL
5"   17"
1" SQS.
C   C
2¼"
TOP
4" RAD.
2¼"
1⅜"
7"   4¼"   10¾"   2"
THREE ½" DIA. HOLES x ⅝" DEEP

4½"
SIDE
24"

SECTION C—C
¾"

TOP DECK
½" DIA. HOLES (3 ON UNDERSIDE)
1" DIA. HOLES (3)
2¼"
2½"
TOP
4" RAD.
2¼"
2½"
8"
2"   2"
2"
13"

SIDE
¾"
21"

SIDE

SIDE
3"

over most surfaces is assured by using a ball for a wheel. A discarded croquet ball can be utilized, or a ball can be glued up and turned as indicated. Start construction by making a pattern from the squared drawing for the horse outlines. Two pieces of 1/2 in. plywood can be tacked or clamped together and cut at the same time to assure the pony sides being identical. Sand off any saw marks and round all edges. Next, cut to size and sand smooth the two wedges that support the axle. Drill a hole in each wedge to provide slight clearances for the 3/4 in. diameter axles. Glue and nail the wedges to the inner surface of each front hoof of the ponies. Sand smooth the two 18 in. lengths of 1 x 1 in. stock for the handles, and attach the handles to the inside surfaces of the ponies with No. 8 x 1 in. flathead screws driven into the handles through holes drilled in the plywood ponies. Countersink the screws and cover the heads. Cut the floor and backboard of the wheelbarrow from 1/2 in. plywood and attach to one pony only, using 1-1/2 in. finishing nails. Set the nails and cover the heads.

Make the ball-shape wheel next, or drill 3/4 in. blind holes in a croquet ball and insert short lengths of 3/4 in. dowel. Dry fit the second side of the wheelbarrow to the assembly and determine how long the dowel axles must be and cut them to length. Paint the ball and let the paint dry thoroughly. In the meantime, paint all parts of the wheelbarrow inside and out, and paint on the ponies' details.

Assemble the second side to the wheelbarrow, at the same time slipping the axles, which have been wiped with wax, into the holes in the wedges. Use glue and finishing nails to attach the second side. Set the nails, fill the holes with wood putty and when it has set, touch up the enamel job. For an added touch of realism, glue short lengths of unraveled rope to the ponies' necks to simulate manes. Strips of plastic can be glued to the ponies' heads to indicate bridles.

Put a smile on a youngster's face with this "two horsepower" wheelbarrow that rolls on a ball-shape wheel.

Prancing Pony Wheelbarrow

Children love both ponies and wheelbarrows, and this interesting toy combines the two. Easy rolling

Cedar Toy Chest

Although this toy box could be made of other materials, cedar was chosen for good reason. The span of time a box is used for toys sometimes is relatively short in terms of the lifetime service a well-crafted chest can provide. Made of cedar, this unit can become a footlocker at the end of a youth bed and eventually be used for blanket and linen storage.

To start construction, edge-glue and dowel the stock to be used for the sides, top and bottom. You may prefer to use plywood for the bottom. When gluing the stock, alternate the grain of every other board. This will minimize warping of the panels.

When the pieces are dry, cut each side panel to the required length and miter each end 45 degrees. Now, using glue and nails or countersunk screws join the ends and sides together. Check for squareness as you assemble the pieces.

Next, check the inside measurements of the chest and cut the bottom to fit. Place the bottom 1/2 in. up from the bottom edge of the chest and secure it in place. For more strength, corner blocks are glued and nailed into each corner.

Now cut the lid to the required dimensions. To increase the rigidity of the lid and prevent it from breaking in the event that some heavyweight sits on it, add two braces to the inside surface. Allow

enough space at the front and back edge of the lid to permit it to close when the braces are attached.

Position the lid on the chest and screw the hinges in place. Now, invert the chest and attach a caster at each corner.

If a finish is desirable, be sure to leave the inside raw wood or hand rub in an oil which won't inhibit the aromatic fragrance of the natural cedar.

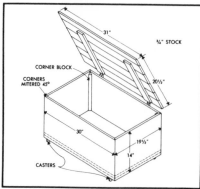

Circus Wagon and Toy Box

Both children and their mothers will like this circus wagon toy box; the kids, because it's a toy they can have fun with and the mothers, because it provides a catch-all for the youngsters' bedroom. Attractive and sturdy enough for even the roughest treatment, the toy box is made of pine with some hardwood used where needed.

Begin by making the two wagon ends, consisting of 1/4 in. plywood panels framed with 3/4 x 2-1/4 in. stock on the sides and bottom and 3/4 in. stock cut on a band saw for the top rail. The frame is assembled with mortise and tenon joints and grooves cut on the inside edges of the frame members to accept the plywood.

Next, the top and bottom side rails are cut to the shape shown and with a 1/4 x 1/4 in. groove sawed their full length. The "bars" are cut from 1/4 x 1 in. hardwood stock, and should fit snugly in the grooves of the rails.

If you are going to paint the toy box with several colors, now would be a good time to paint some of the pieces separately. Initially, all pieces are given a coat of clear sealer and then coats of nontoxic enamel are applied.

While the paint is drying, turn the four axles on a lathe from some straight-grained hardwood to the dimensions and profile given. Sand them smooth, apply a coat of clear sealer and set them aside to dry.

Next, make the handle and turning mechanism for the front wheels. Cut the two front wheel blocks and the handle blocks from hardwood to the shape and dimensions shown. The handle and the front axle spacer also are cut from hardwood, and the six pieces are assembled with glue and screws. When attaching the handle to the handle blocks with the dowel, be careful not to get glue inside the hole in the handle. Glue the dowel only to the blocks so the handle can be moved vertically. Cut the turning plates and the turning-plate stretcher, drill the hole for the carriage bolt and check to see that all the pieces align well and work smoothly.

Cut the rear axle blocks and the floor support cleats. Attach the cleats to the sides with glue and screws, and you're ready to assemble the main body of the wagon. Attach the ends to the sides with glue and screws, but be sure to use finishing washers for a smooth surface. Fit the rear wheel axle blocks to the sides and attach the front wheel block/turning mechanism to the turning stretcher.

Now is the time to decide what kind of wheels to use. The original was made with hardwood wheels turned to the dimensions shown and painted gloss black. If you don't want to go to the trouble of turning wheels, you can purchase ready-made units from a hardware store. Plastic or metal wheels are an alternative, but you will have to make the appropriate changes in the axles that will be used. With any type of wheels, a bolt can be substituted for the wooden axle. After the wheels are on and turning smoothly, cut a piece of 1/4 in. hardboard for the floor and glue it to the cleats.

Finish by sanding and painting as desired and inspect thoroughly for any flaws that might be harmful to children. One last note: if you're going to use wooden wheels and axles, rub some paraffin on the contacting surfaces to reduce friction and assure smooth rotation.

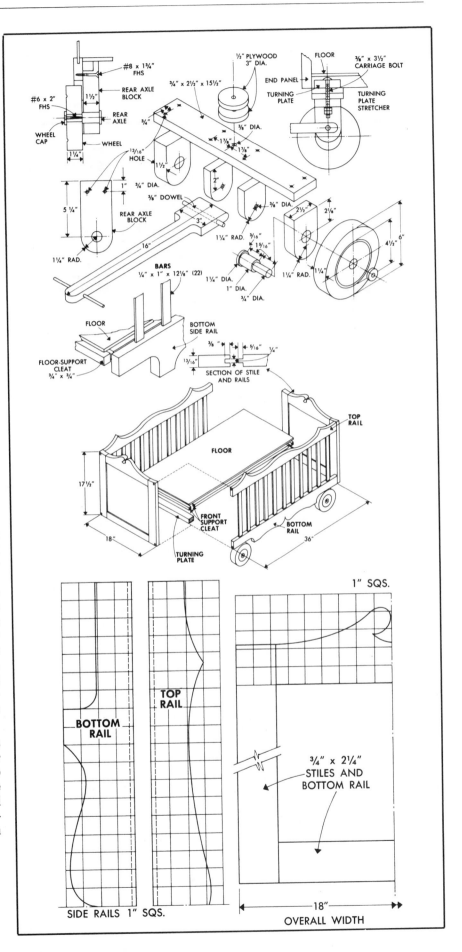

Two Locomotive Toy Boxes

Big enough to play inside and with ample storage room for toys, these locomotives will delight any young Casey Jones. One of the locomotives is for steam fans, the other is a more modern diesel switch engine. Both cabs are identical, but the undercarriage, wheel assemblies and forward part of the units are different.

Assembly has been kept as simple as possible; the only problem might be in making the wheels. They can be rough cut on a bandsaw, then taken to someone who has a lathe and finish cut. Rubber-tired wheels for wagons, tricycles and the like, of approximately this size, also could be used. The railing around the engine of the diesel is made of 6 in. lengths of 1/2 in. dowel, drilled to accept lengths of 1/8 in. dowel.

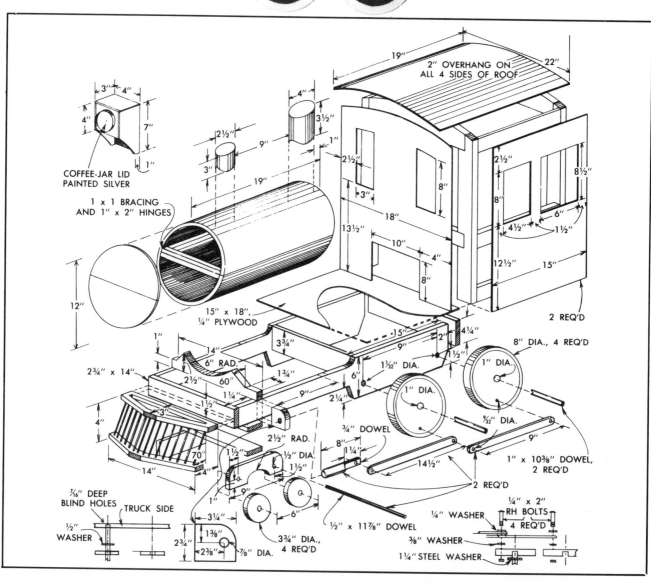

The paint job can be varied to suit the builder's fancy.

The boiler on the steam unit and the engine compartment on the diesel unit are used for toy storage. A framework of 1 x 2s is suggested for the fiberboard drum used for the boiler of the steam locomotive, while the top of the engine compartment on the diesel simply can be fitted with hinges to convert it to a toy box.

All parts of either locomotive should be well sealed to protect against weather before they are painted, as no doubt they will spend some time outdoors. Although not shown, a simple box seat fitted with a cushion could be located on either side of the locomotive cab so that the "engineer" and the "fireman" can each be seated, as in a real locomotive.

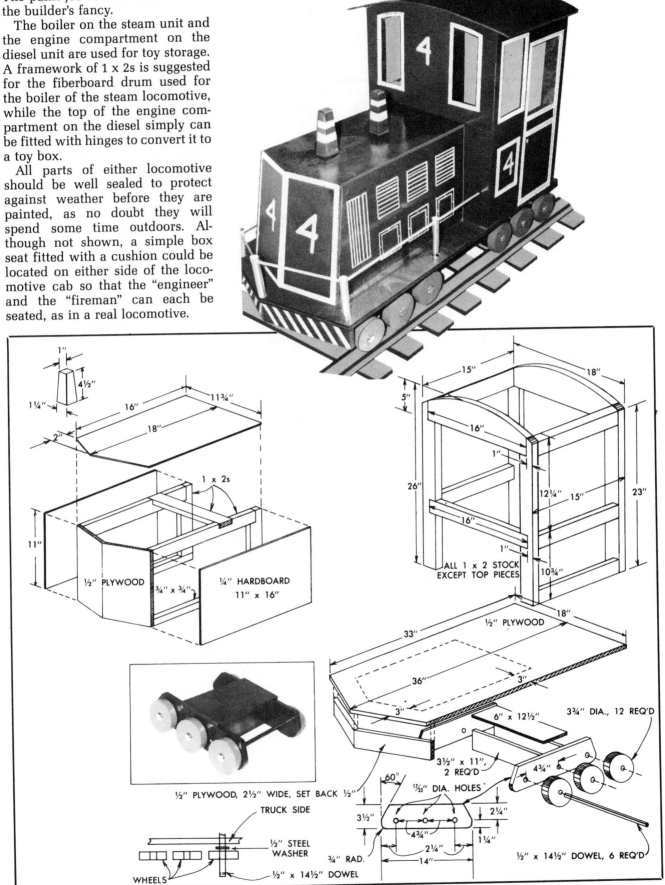

This child size boxcar is really a heavy-duty toy box that can be easily rolled about on eight working wheels. The car is basically a plywood box assembled on a 1/2 in. plywood base. The side and end pieces are cut from 1/2 in. plywood to the dimensions given. The slanted roof frame is assembled from 1 in. stock then covered with 1/4 in. hardboard so that the roof overhangs all around. The roof frame is attached to the sides and ends of the car.

Sliding doors of 1/4 in. plywood give easy access to the roomy interior. The 8-1/2 in. doors slide in grooves in the floor and roof members. The door opening is 16 in. wide.

Each wheel truck consists of two hardwood sides and a T-shape crosspiece assembled as shown. Cut truck sides from 3/4 in. hardwood to 3 x 9 in. and shape as shown. Assemble the trucks as indicated.

Wooden wheels, turned on a lathe, were used in the original, but metal or plastic wheels also could be used. The axles are hardwood dowels coated with paste-wax for non-squeak running. If the wheels you use are different in diameter it may be necessary to re-design the side members of the trucks to provide proper clearance. Also, while both trucks are shown to be fixed solidly, you may wish to pivot one truck so that the car could be steered around corners. To make a pivot, use a 1/4 in. bolt with a flat washer between the frame and truck to assure easier pivoting.

Fixed trucks are attached to the floor of the car with two 1-1/2 in. steel screws. The trucks are attached 6 in. from each end of the car.

The catwalk on the roof is made from four hardwood planks attached to five saddles placed equal distances apart. The saddles are made from softwood, V-notched to fit the roof. When spacing the saddles allow the catwalk a 2 in. overhang at each end.

The end and side trim bracing is made of softwood and adds an air of authenticity. The H-shape on the end measures 4 in. across as shown.

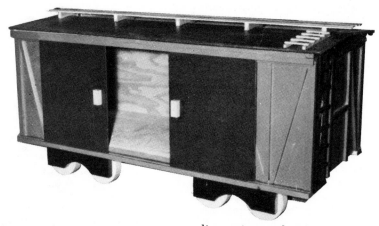

Boxcar Toy Box

The finishing touches for the car are the two vertical access ladders and two roof ladders made to the dimensions shown. For a paint scheme consult your junior railroader or adhere to traditional train colors: red car, black ladders and wheels, brown doors, natural catwalk and red or orange truck sides.

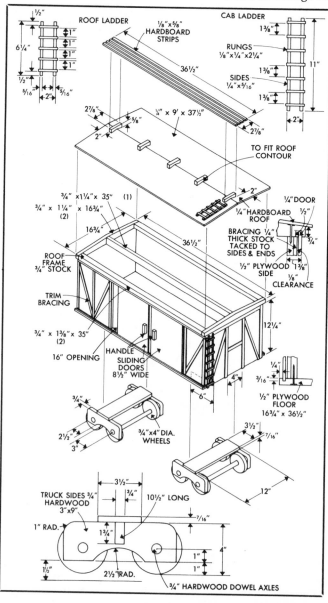

Tank Car Toy Box

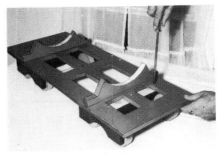

Little boys are fascinated by this model railroad tank car that really rolls on its own wheels and doesn't look at all like a container for toys. The youngster can have all kinds of fun wheeling the tank car to where the soldiers and blocks are scattered.

Obtain a cylindrical pasteboard container about 10 in. in diameter from a local merchant for the tank. It will be necessary to cut disks of 3/4 in. plywood to fit in the ends of the container to strengthen it. Cut through the container 4 in. from each end down to the center, then longitudinally to create a "lid" as shown in the drawing. Another 10 in. disk of plywood is cut in half and the halves screwed to the ends of the lid to reinforce it. Use round-head screws to create the appearance of roundhead rivets. Rip strips 1 in. wide from 1 in. solid stock and fit the strips between the half disks of the lid. Attach them to the edges of the lid with roundhead screws. Similar strips are fitted inside the edges of the cutout in the container to reinforce it. A fourth 10 in. disk is cut in half, then sawed to produce half rings 1-1/2 in. wide that are fitted in the ends of the cutout in the container to strengthen the edges. Attach them with roundhead wood screws.

If you cannot obtain a cylindrical container, make the tank from a wooden framework covered with do-it-yourself sheet aluminum that can be purchased at hardware stores. Two disks cut from 3/4 in. plywood, two half-disks and two half rings, as used in the container, are used. The main difference is that the strips on the edges of the

cutout are lengthened and run from end to end of the tank. They are glued and screwed to the end disks. A third stringer is run from end to end, and is positioned at what will be the center of the bottom of the tank. The sheet aluminum is readily wrapped around this framework and is easily cut with tin snips or with heavy-duty scissors. Use roundhead wood screws to simulate roundhead rivets to attach the aluminum, spacing the screws equidistant around the end disks and along the reinforcing stringers. One very real advantage of building the tank with sheet aluminum is that the material already has a shiny metallic finish and needs only a stripe of bright color around each end to look much like a genuine railroad tank car. The pasteboard container first will have to be shellacked, then coated with aluminum paint. The two coatings will be required both to make the tank look realistic and to protect it against wear and tear.

The "frame" under the tank is a rectangle cut from 3/4 in. plywood as indicated in the drawing. The quickest, easiest way to make the cutouts in the frame is with a saber saw. The tank supports are made

next. These can be cut from 1 in. solid stock or 3/4 in. plywood. Solid stock is preferred in this instance as it will provide better holding properties for the screws. Attach the tank supports with glue and screws, then attach the tank with screws driven from inside. If your youngster is liable to climb inside the tank to play, it would be a good idea to provide a third tank support under the center.

The trucks are cut out and assembled as indicated. Wooden wheels, turned on a lathe, were used on the original trucks. The axles are wooden dowels. You may wish to use metal wheels. If wheels of a different diameter are used it may be necessary to redesign the side members of the trucks to provide proper clearance. Also, while both trucks are shown to be fixed solidly to the frame with glue and screws, you may wish to pivot one truck. Then a simple handle could be attached to the truck to enable a youngster to steer. Use a 1/4 in. nut and bolt for the pivot, with a flat washer between the frame and truck.

The ladder is assembled from dowels, the vertical members being 3/8 in., the rungs 1/8 in. Note that the holes for the ladder ends in the frame are angled more than necessary. When the ladder is forced into these holes it is held firmly against the tank and cannot readily be removed.

The tank lid now is hinged to the tank, and a stop-chain is fitted on each side to prevent the lid from falling all the way back and tearing the hinges loose. The "dome" on the tank is made from a cylindrical box, such as used to package salt or oatmeal. Hold the box vertically at the center of the lid and mark around it with a pencil held on a block of wood. Cut along the marked line. The odd-shaped strip

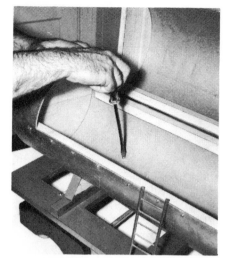

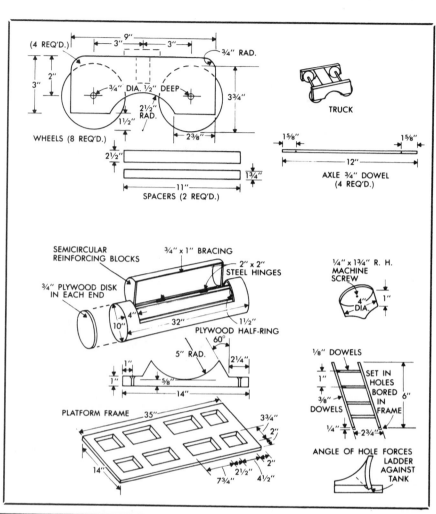

(4 REQ'D.)

WHEELS (8 REQ'D.)

3/4" DIA. 1/2" DEEP

2 1/2" RAD.

1 1/2"

2 3/8"

3/4" RAD.

3 3/4"

SPACERS (2 REQ'D.)

2 1/2"

1 3/4"

11"

TRUCK

1 5/8" 1 5/8"

12"

AXLE 3/4" DOWEL
(4 REQ'D.)

SEMICIRCULAR
REINFORCING BLOCKS

3/4" PLYWOOD DISK
IN EACH END

3/4" x 1" BRACING

2" x 2"
STEEL HINGES

4"

10"

32"

1 1/2"

PLYWOOD HALF-RING

5" RAD. 60°

1"
1"

5/8"

2 1/4"

14"

PLATFORM FRAME

35"

3 3/4"
2"

14"

7 3/4" 2 1/2" 4 1/2"

2"

1/4" x 1 3/4" R. H.
MACHINE
SCREW

4"
DIA.

1"

1/8" DOWELS

SET IN
HOLES
BORED
IN
FRAME

6"

1"

3/8"
DOWELS

1/4" 2 3/4"

ANGLE OF HOLE FORCES
LADDER
AGAINST
TANK

removed now can be used as a pattern and is positioned 1 in. from the top of the box. Mark along the pattern, then cut the dome. Attach it to the center of the top of the lid with a 1/4 in. nut and bolt. Use a flat washer under the head of the bolt and under the nut.

The paint colors used on the tank car can be as varied as you wish, as children love bright colors. The original had a silver tank, the frame was brown, bands on the tank were black, the ladder was bright green, the trucks black and the wheels bright orange.

Caboose Toy Box

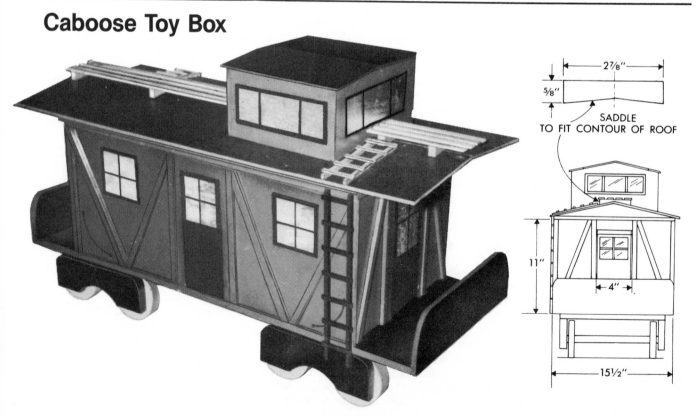

2 7/8"

5/8"

SADDLE
TO FIT CONTOUR OF ROOF

11"

4"

15 1/2"

Next to the engine, the car on a train that most interests youngsters is the caboose. It is from here that the conductor directs operations and watches over the long string of freight cars that run from the caboose to the engine. The cupola on top of the caboose is to permit the conductor to see the cars ahead.

This replica of a caboose has a roof that hinges open to permit the storage of toys. Hardwood wheels allow the box to be moved around.

Start construction by cutting the ends, sides and floor of the main cab from 1/2 in. plywood. Also cut the guards that fit at the ends of the platforms, and rip 1/2 in. strips from 1/4 in. plywood to create the bracing that is attached to the cab sides. The bracing on the ends of the caboose is cut 3/4 in. wide. Use glue and finishing nails to assemble the caboose and to attach the bracing.

The two trucks are made next. Those on the model shown are fixed, but a pivot could be fitted in one set of trucks to allow the assembly to turn. To steer the caboose, a handle could be fitted to the truck.

Members of the roof framing are ripped from 1 in. stock (3/4 in. net)

and assembled with glue and finishing nails as indicated. Cut the two pieces of hardboard that cover the framework and attach them. Round the edges of the hardboard to eliminate any sharp corners.

Cut the ends and sides of the cupola next. The lower edges of the sides will have to be cut at an angle to match that of the roof of the cab. Check the angle of the roof and match the V-notch of the cupola ends to it.

The cupola is assembled with glue and finishing nails. The hardboard pieces for the roof are cut to size and attached. Attach the cupola to the roof by driving screws up through the hardboard of the roof into the sides and ends of the cupola.

Before putting the catwalks on the roof, paint the roof black or red. When the paint has dried, attach the five saddles, three for the longer catwalk, two for the shorter portion. They are attached by driving screws up through the car's roof. Paint the saddles and the planks for the walks before assembling the walks on the roof. Now glue and nail the planks to the saddles. Also attach the roof planks, which also

should be painted before they are attached.

When attaching the bracing strips on the car's sides and ends, use short brads and glue. Inspect the inside carefully to make sure that none of the brads project through inside. If any do, use two hammers and peen the sharp ends back.

After painting the ends and sides of the caboose and cupola a bright red or yellow, the windows and doors are marked in. Brush or spray the area of the glass with a silver paint, then when it is dry, mask the area and paint in the door and window frame details.

The ladders for the roof and side now are assembled, painted, then fastened in place. The last step is to hinge the roof to the sides of the caboose. Also use a length of chain or a lid support to prevent the top from falling back too far.

The "Grab Bars" at the lower corners of the sides are painted on with black enamel. It is not suggested that they actually be made and attached, as they could be "leg bruisers" for youngsters and would serve no practical purpose. Be sure to use nontoxic paints.

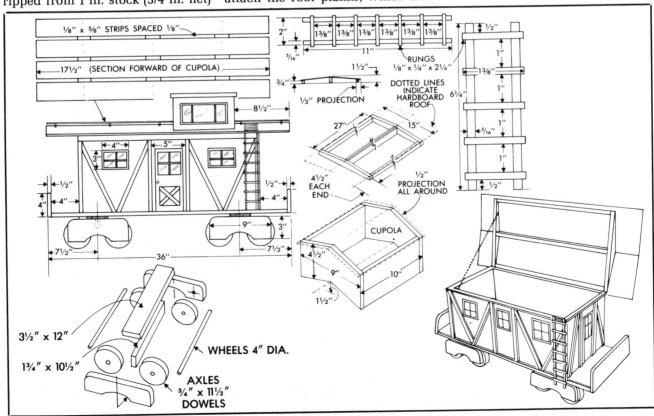

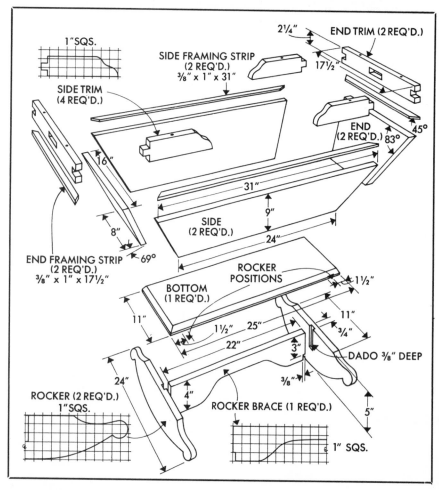

Pioneer Cradle

Destined to become an heirloom itself, this charming cradle is patterned after a century-old home-built model that was found in the attic of a farmhouse.

The cradle shown was built from 1 in. spruce (3/4 in. net), treated with fruitwood stain, then given three coats of clear plastic, satin finish. Pine or any other lumber also could be used.

Start construction by cutting all four edges of the cradle bottom at 62 degrees. Edge-glued stock can be used for the bottom, or you can use a piece of 3/4 in. plywood. With plywood, cut the bottom 1-1/2 in. shorter in length and width, then add 3/4 in. molding, rather than beveling edges as with lumber.

Cut the top and bottom edges of the cradle sides and ends at 69 degrees, the edges of the same pieces at 83 degrees. Assemble the sides and ends with glue and screws in counterbored holes that can be plugged or filled.

Cut and miter the four pieces of trim that fit on the upper edges of the ends and sides. Glue and nail it in place on the upper edges, keeping the outer edges flush with the outer surfaces of the cradle body.

Next step is to cut to size and shape the two end and four side pieces that fit on the upper edges of the cradle at the ends. Use glue and

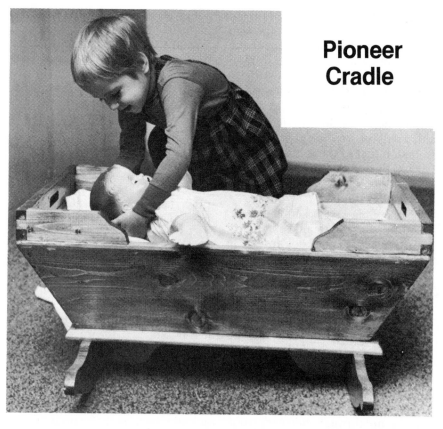

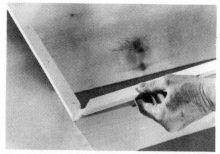

Four top framing strips are mitered at the corners, glued and nailed into place flush with outer surfaces of cradle sides.

End pieces are cut to size and shape, hand holes cut and filed, then pieces are attached to ends with screws.

screws in counterbored holes to attach these six pieces to the cradle. Firm attachment is necessary, as the hand holes in the end pieces are used to lift the cradle.

Cut the rockers to shape, then make the blind mortise at the center of each rocker to accept the tenons on the ends of the stretcher that braces the bottom assembly. Use glue and nails to join the rockers and brace, then attach this assembly to the cradle bottom with screws driven down through the bottom.

Open tenons of side pieces are slipped into end pieces, then side pieces are attached with screws.

Tenons on ends of brace are fitted into blind mortises at the midpoints of the rockers, held with glue and nails.

Cradle bottom is screwed to rocker-brace assembly, then bottom is attached to cradle sides and ends with screws.

Finally, turn the cradle body upside down and attach the rocker-bottom assembly to the ends and sides with flathead screws. Countersink the screws well, but they need not be plugged or filled as they will not be seen.

Smooth, sand and fill all surfaces and defects, as well as over countersunk nails and screws that can be seen. Finally, apply your finish.

Swinging Doll Cradle

Almost any little girl would be happy to have this swinging cradle to help put to sleep a cranky doll. Dad or grandfather will appreciate the fact that stock 1 x 4s, 2 x 4s and 1 x 12 shelving, all No. 2 pine, plus some 1/2 and 5/8 in. dowels are all that are required, which makes the project quite inexpensive to build. Additionally you will need to buy, whittle or turn a wooden drawer pull that is used to make the lock for the cradle.

The lock keeps the cradle from swinging, so it can be used for changing diapers and other tasks.

Start construction by assembling the stand that supports the cradle. Cut the end posts, Parts A, after first making a pattern by enlarging the squared half drawing. A notch 3/4 x 1-1/16 in. is cut at the bottom corners to create a tenon.

Next, shape the two "feet." They can be simple strips with the ends rounded or as fancy as you wish. At the center of each foot mark and cut a mortise to accept the tenons on the bottoms of the end posts. Make the mortises a bit undersize, then gradually enlarge them to create a snug fit for the tenons on the posts.

Bore blind holes 5/8 in. in diameter and 9/16 in. deep on the inner face of each post, as shown in the drawing. While the locations of the holes need not be exactly as shown, both holes must be in identical locations to assure the dowel brace being level and on center.

Glue the dowel brace in the blind holes, then position the scrolled stretcher, Part C, centered on top of the feet. Clamp this assembly, square it up and let the glue set at least overnight. Drive small finishing nails through the posts into the dowel brace and the stretcher.

While the glue on the stand is set-

ting, cut out and assemble the cradle. Cut the ends, Parts E, from the 1 x 12 shelving. This will require first making a pattern by enlarging the squared drawing. Incidentally, although not previously mentioned, a pattern from the squared drawing also is required for the stretcher, Part C.

Stand for cradle consists of uprights with "feet," scrolled stretcher and dowel brace fitted in holes in uprights.

Side rails, Parts F, of which four are required, are cut from lengths of 5/8 in. dowel. Lay out and drill the seven 3/8 in. holes for the dowel spindles, plus the three in each bottom rail for the bottom dowel supports. Note that the holes for the bottom dowels are at an angle of about 103 degrees in relation to the side spindles. The angle may vary slightly, depending on your assembly, but the spindles should be parallel to the angled edges of the cradle ends.

Bore four blind holes on the inside surface of each end for the rails, and the through hole for the 1/2 x 2-1/2 in. dowel that supports the cradle in the stand. Glue together the side rails, spindles and bottom dowels, then glue this assembly into the two cradle ends.

Make sure the hole in each cradle end is a sliding fit for the dowel, while the hole in each post should be snug. Tap the dowels through the cradle ends into the holes in the posts, with glue in the post holes. Also drive a screw through the side of each post, into the dowel to prevent its turning.

Make the cradle lock as detailed, then drill through one end post and through the cradle end so the lock can be fitted in place. It would not be a bad idea to fasten a light chain to the lock and cradle post to prevent the lock from being mislaid.

When the glue has set, cut a scrap of hardboard, plywood or particleboard for the cradle bottom and drop into place.

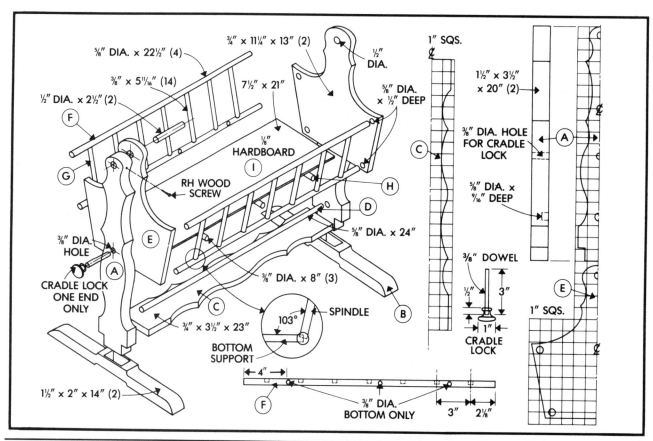

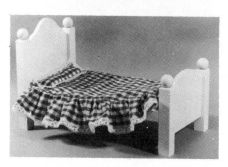

Doll Size Bedroom Furniture

This enchanting bedroom set, proportioned for dolls up to 14 in. tall, consists of four pieces: wardrobe, bed, dressing table and bench seat.

One of the nice things about this project is that it can be made from scraps found in almost any woodworker's shop.

Wardrobe

The basic cabinet and doors are made from 1/2 in. solid stock. You might use softwood and paint it,

but hardwood can be used if the piece is to be stained and varnished or lacquered. As an alternative use 1/2 in. hardwood-plywood and cover the edge grain with veneer tape.

The back of the wardrobe, and the backup panels for the door, are cut from 1/8 in. hardboard or plywood.

Start construction with the doors, first making the cutouts, then shaping the outside. Sand both inside and outside edges glass-smooth. Remember that in a scaled down piece of furniture any saw marks or rough spots are even more noticeable than on full size furniture.

Next, cut the 1/8 in. hardboard backup panels 1/4 in. longer and wider than the opening in each door. Cut these panels after you have made the cutouts to allow for any variation in size from the dimensions shown.

This will assure a 1/8 in. overlap on all four sides of the opening. Wrap fabric around the backup panels and glue to the back. You might use scraps for this, and the matching spread on the bed and the pillow on the stool.

Attach the panels inside the doors with very small roundhead screws or small nails. This will permit easy removal of the panels so the material can be changed at some future date. The panels also should be removed when the wardrobe is painted or stained and finished.

Assemble the rest of the wardrobe with glue and brads, then install the shelves and clothes rod. Paint or finish all parts, then hang the doors with 3/4 x 1 in. butt hinges. A 1/8 x 5/8 in. strip on the right door holds both to the cabinet. Make sure the right door drags slightly to act as a catch.

Dressing Table and Stool

The dressing table is easily assembled from 1/2 or 3/8 in. stock, with a cutout in the front to accept a drawer. The drawer will take a bit of precise fitting, and has sides, front and back made of 1/4 in. stock with the bottom 1/8 in. hardboard. Note that the drawer has a "false front" cut from 1/4 in. stock to lap all around.

The top and bottom drawer guides are strips of 1/4 x 1/4 in. solid stock positioned just above and just below the opening for the drawer.

The mirror supports are 3/8 x 3/4 in. strips 6 in. long. The mirror frame is 1/4 in. plywood or solid stock. The dresser shown has a "mirror" of aluminum foil glued to the frame. A scrap of lightweight mirror could be cut to size and recessed into the frame for a more realistic appearance.

The bench seat for the dressing table is a scaled down version of the table and should offer no difficulties in assembling. One change you might want to make is to hinge the top of the seat and create a small storage space under it. This would require installing a bottom of 1/8 in. hardboard also. The bottom could be fitted in grooves cut on the inner surfaces of the four sides, or small cleats could be glued and bradded inside to support it.

Bed

About the only items you won't have in the scrap box for making the bed are the round balls on the tops of the corner posts. These were purchased at a craft shop and

come in a variety of sizes. If you are a lathe buff, the spheres could be easily turned.

Attach the balls with a small dowel; the wooden beads you buy in a hobby shop will already have holes in them and you simply glue a dowel in the hole, and in a hole bored in the top of each bedpost.

A mattress can be fashioned from a piece of scrap foam rubber or urethane fitted in a cloth sleeve made to fit it. Pillows could be made the same way.

No instructions are given for the spread or pillow on the bed or the pillow on the stool. That is left to the discretion of the builder.

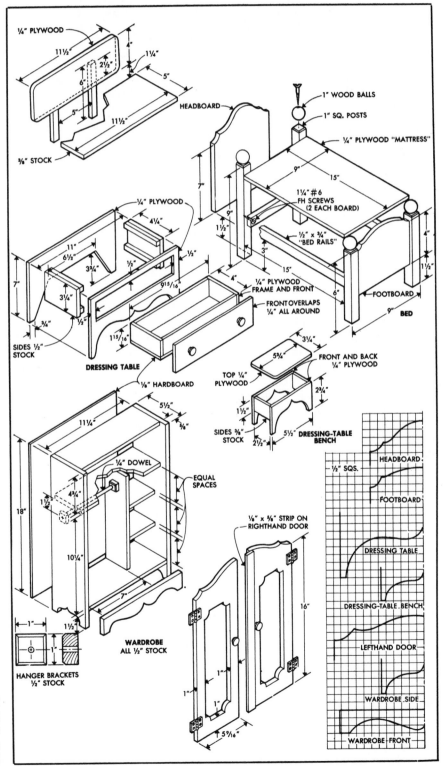

The Borden Dollhouse

(with some modifications by the WORKBENCH editors)

For the "build-it-from-scratch" craftsman this dollhouse as shown in the Borden glue ads can be a satisfying project. It isn't really as complicated as it looks, but there are a lot of pieces and parts, so take your time and allow the glue to set completely on one setup before you begin the next. If you don't, you are liable to damage the part already done, as well as the one you are trying to add.

Rather than having just one Materials List, there are several, each located near the portion of the house being discussed. First, to assemble the basic house you will need the following:

Roof, Walls, 1/4″ x 4′ x 8′ A-C plywood (1)
Floors, 3/8″ x 4′ x 4′ A-C plywood (1)
Trim A, 1/16″ x 3/8″ x 24″ (22)
    B, 3/16″ x 1/4″ x 24″ (6)
    C, 1/16″ x 1-1/2″ x 24″ (2)
    D, 1-1/4″ x 12″ fluted molding (1) (or make your own fascia trim)
Siding, 1/16″ x 1/2″ x 24″ (70) Or purchase 3-1/2″ x 22″ sheets of ready made siding
Shingles, cut from wooden tongue depressors, or from 1/8 in.

strips of softwood. Or purchase ready made shingles from dollhouse suppliers, 100 to a bag, two bags required.
Miscellaneous supplies needed:
White glue, carpenter's glue, contact adhesive, wood filler, paint, masking tape, sandpaper and 1 in. brads.

Start by cutting three 13 x 48 in. pieces from the 3/8 in. plywood for the floors. On one, mark the basic floor plan and the locations of the partitions, Fig. 1. When you have one sheet marked, tack nail or clamp the three pieces together and carefully cut them to shape so they all are identical.

Next, cut the walls and roofs to size and shape, Figs. 2, 3, 4 and 5. Note that the openings for doors and windows are sized for the make-your-own doors and windows described later. If you want to use ready made units from dollhouse suppliers, size them to fit. It's best to actually have the doors and windows on hand before you cut the openings.

Be sure to cut the proper number of pieces of each of the shapes in Figs. 2, 3, 4 and 5. The numbers in parentheses, such as (2), indicate the number of pieces to be cut.

As you lay out the locations of

window and door openings also mark the positions of the second floor and attic floor. Make sure the marks are on the inside surfaces of the various pieces. The "good" or "A" side of the plywood should be on the inside, while the "C" or "poor" side is on the outside where it will be covered by the siding.

Also, when making wall and roof pieces that are in pairs, as "D" in Fig. 3 and "Z" in Fig. 5, clamp the plywood with the "A" sides together. Roof pieces also have the "A" side inward (down) because the roof shingles will cover the rougher "C" side of the plywood.

After all the pieces have been cut to size and shape, check all edges for voids and all surface areas for dents or scratches. Use wood filler and a putty knife to fill voids and imperfections, let dry, then sand smooth.

Fast-tack carpenter's glue and 1 in. brads are used for the assembly of the dollhouse. After the brads are driven, immediately wipe off any excess glue with a damp cloth. If you miss any of the glue, it can be scraped off after it dries with a sharp wood chisel. Once you have glued up an assembly, let it stand for at least 12 hours to make sure the glue has set completely.

If you have bar clamps they certainly would be a help in making the dollhouse, but if you don't have clamps the glue and brads will hold the pieces in place until the glue sets. One help is to apply the carpenter's glue, then expose it to the air for about 30 seconds. It will set up slightly for a faster "grab" and the pieces being joined will not move easily.

Carefully examine Fig. 6 to see how the various components are joined in the assembly. Start by attaching wall sections "B" to the first floor, then add front wall "A" and sections "C" and "D." Glue and brad interior walls "E" to the first floor and to the edges of walls "B."

Next, glue and brad interior walls "F" on top of the second floor, where you marked the locations. Clamp blocks on one or both sides of the walls to keep them square with the floor and let the glue set completely. When the glue has set, slip the floor/walls assembly into

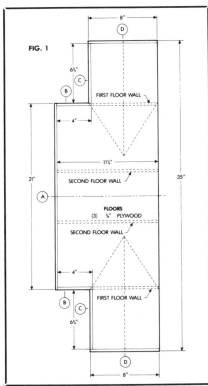

FIG. 1

the house on top of the first floor interior walls. Mark along the top and bottom of the floor and on each side of the walls, on the outside walls of the house, then remove the assembly. Apply a thin line of glue along between the marks, then install the floor/walls assembly and brad it where possible.

As indicated at the top of Fig. 4, gluing and bradding a small crown or cove molding on the walls will provide additional support and nailing surfaces for the floors.

Insert the attic floor, mark the edges on the walls, remove and apply glue, then fit the floor in place. Let the basic house assembly set at least 12 hours after the last glue is applied to make sure the structure is solid.

Attach the roof beginning with center sections "Y." To assure a rigid assembly during construction, make a temporary back gable "X" the same size and shape as the upper, angled portion of front wall "A." Glue and brad the two "Y" roof pieces to the top of wall "A" and clamp or loosely brad the temporary gable at the other ends of the "Y" roof members.

Position each of the four roof pieces "Z" against the "Y" roof members and mark along the underside on the "Y" pieces. Posi-

tion one piece at a time and remove it and set it aside. Now, cut and attach the four 1/8 x 1/8 x 4 in. support strips with glue, under the lines made to mark the locations of the "Z" pieces. At this point, let the house set for 12 hours to allow the glue to set up completely.

At the next work session, use glue and brads to attach roof sections "Z." The basic house is finished and ready for the "finishing touches." If you don't want to apply siding, use filler to fill in any defects, let it dry, then sand smooth. Paint a suitable color.

You can buy ready-made siding in panels, or cut your own from 1/16 x 1/2 x 24 in. strips of balsa or other wood. Start at the bottoms of the walls and overlap each preceding strip by about 1/8 in.

Roof shingles can be purchased, or you can cut 1/4 x 3/4 in. pieces from 1/8 in. lattice stock. If trim on the house is to be a contrasting color, paint it before attaching it to the already painted house. The trim strips can be bradded on over the siding, but a more professional look will be achieved by installing the trim strips first, then prepainting

the siding, cutting it to butt against the trim, then touching up the paint where necessary with a tiny brush. The molding strips "A" are indicated in Fig. 7 as to location, including those on each side of the ridge of the roof. The latter is attached over the shingles. When all this work is done, remove the temporary gable "X."

Brackets that fit against the fascia and up against the underside of the roof overhang are 1/2 in. slices cut from small molding, with the tops beveled to fit against the roof.

While only one bay window is shown on the house, Fig. 8, you might want two, one for each end. In this case, double the number of pieces in the Materials List.

Bay Window Materials List
a, 1-15/16" x 5-1/4" clear plastic (3)
b, c, d, e and f are dimensioned on
  drawing, with number required
g, 1/8" x 1/4" x 1-7/16" (6)
h, 1/8" x 1/4" x 5-1/4" (6)
i, 1/8" x 1/8" x 1-7/16" (3)
j, 1/8" x 1/8" x 3/4" (6)

The edges of parts "e" and "f" are beveled with sandpaper, as are the edges of the six "h" strips that meet to form the bay and contact the

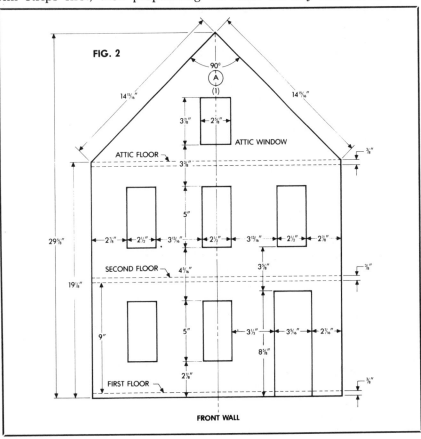

FIG. 2

FRONT WALL

wall. If any joints do not meet exactly, fill voids with filler, let it dry and sand smooth. The clear plastic is glued to the backs of the three windows in the bay.

There are 12 "regular" windows and one for the attic. All windows have a pair of shutters, but the attic window does not have the detailed cornice above as do the other windows. Note that the trim for the windows goes both inside and outside of the window openings.

Materials List for Windows and Shutters

a, 1/8" x 1/2" x 4" (12)
b, 3/8" x 3/8" x 3-1/2" (12)
c, 1/4" x 1/4" x 3-1/4" (48)
d, 1/8" x 1/8" x 2-7/8" (24)
e, 1/8" x 3/8" x 4-3/4" (48)
f, 1/8" x 1/8" x 2-1/16" (12)
g, 1/16" x 3/16" x 1-1/4" (50)
h, 1/16" x 3/16" x 4-1/4" (48)
i, 1/16" x 1-1/4" x 4-5/8" (24)
j, 1/8" x 3/8" x 3-3/8" (4)
k, 1/8" x 3/8" x 3-5/8" (4)
l, 1/16" x 3/16" x 3" (4)
m, 1/16" x 1-1/4" x 3-3/8" (2)

After cutting the various pieces to size, lightly mark them with a pencil so you can tell which is the a, b, c, etc., then place them in separate piles. This way you can more easily select the proper pieces to position and glue around the window openings.

One quick and accurate method of assembling the windows is to use a softwood board covered with waxed paper. Position the various pieces for each window and hold them in place with pins or push pins while the glue sets. There will be some glue squeeze-out, but the waxed paper will prevent the assembly from sticking to the board, and excess glue can be removed with a razor knife and the joints sanded smooth.

Make "sandwiches" of parts b, c, b and d for the top of the bay, and parts d and b for the bottom, gluing the pieces together and wiping off excess glue after the pieces are clamped together.

When the glue has set for a few hours (the longer the better), glue the three windows between the top and bottom, angled as shown. When the glue has set on this assembly, add parts "e" for the roof and parts "f" for the bottom. When

the glue has set for at least 12 hours, attach the bay window to the opening on the house.

The regular windows, attic window and the shutters are assembled in much the same fashion as the individual windows for the bay, using a board covered with waxed paper. When all the frames are assembled and the glue has set, install them inside and outside the window openings as indicated. Clear plastic is indicated for the windows and will create a more authentic appearance, but can be eliminated if you wish.

The very attractive door for the dollhouse, Fig. 9, is assembled from a number of pieces, as is the facade that fits along both sides and over the top.

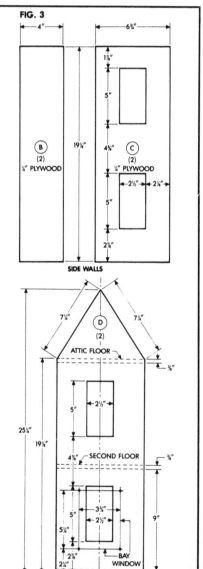

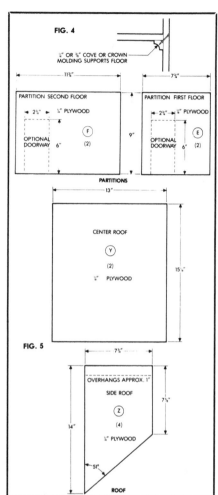

Materials List for Door

a, 1/8" x 5/8" x 4-3/8" (2)
b, 1/2" x 9/16" x 13/16" (2)
c, 1/8" x 3/4" x 4-5/8" (1)
d, 1/2" x 9/16" x 1-1/4" (2)
e, 1/8" x 1/2" x 5-9/16" (2)
f, 1/4" x 5/8" x 3/4" (2)
g, 1/8" x 3/8" x 3-1/8" (1)
h, 1/4" x 1" x 1-15/16" (2)
hh, 1/4" x 1" x 1-1/2" (2)
i, 1/4" x 1" x 1-3/16" (2)
j, 1/4" x 1" x 1-3/8" (2)
k, 1/8" x 3/16" x 2-15/16" (1)
l, 1/8" x 1/2" x 2-15/16" (1)
m, 1/8" x 3/16" x 8-5/8" (2)
n, 3/32" x 1/2" x 1-13/16" (4)
o, 3/32" x 1/2" x 3/4" (1)
p, 3/32" x 1/2" x 2" (2)
q, 3/32" x 1/2" x 6-7/8" (2)
r, 1/8" x 3/8" x 2-15/16" (1)
s, 1/4" x 2-7/8" x 6-7/8" (1)

Use the board with waxed paper method as for the windows and assemble the facade and door. If you want the door to open, build the door separate from the facade and hinge it to the facade. It will have to swing inward, of course, as the facade would prevent it opening out. Exterior doors on full size houses almost always open inward. Storm sash and screen doors open outward.

While assembling the bay window, the regular windows and the door and facade, paint them before attaching them to the house if they are to be a different color than the house. Don't, of course, paint the interior window trim.

The basic dollhouse now is complete and ready for interior decorating and furnishing. As carpenter and contractor your job is finished and the rest is up to the new owner.

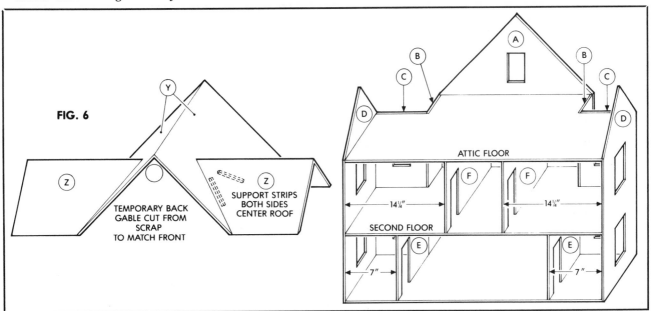

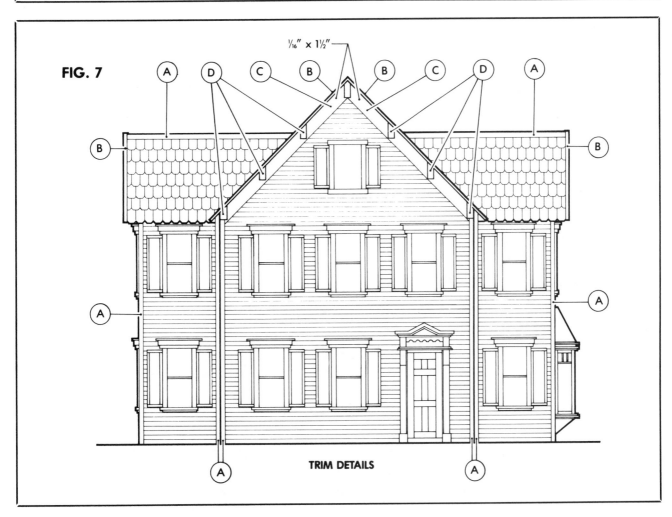

TRIM DETAILS

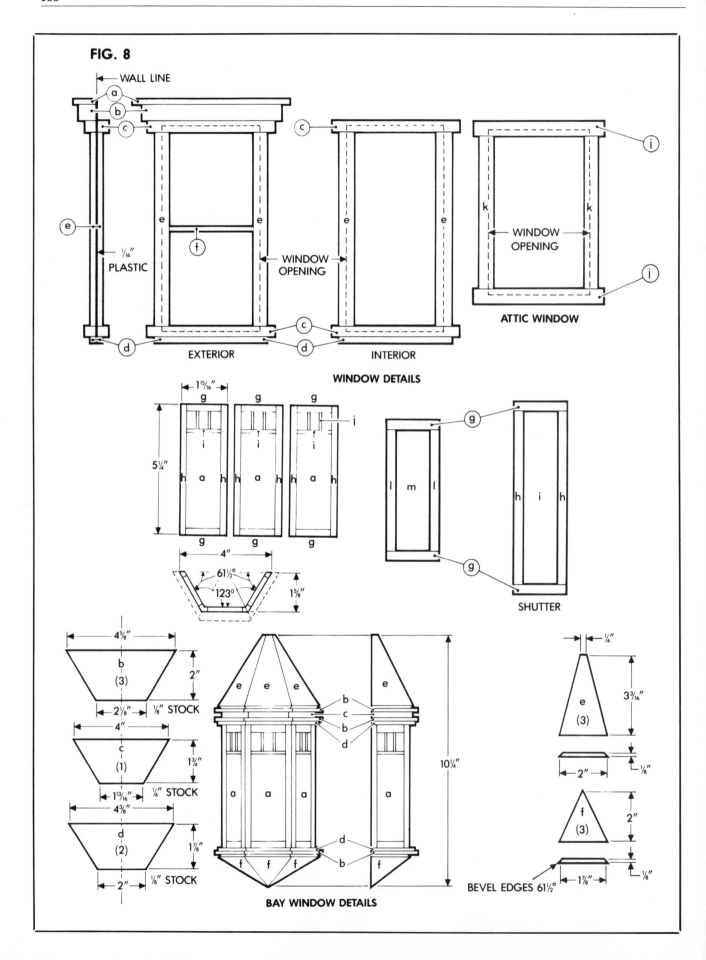

FIG. 8

WALL LINE

1/16" PLASTIC

PLASTIC

WINDOW OPENING

EXTERIOR

WINDOW OPENING

INTERIOR

WINDOW DETAILS

WINDOW OPENING

ATTIC WINDOW

1 15/16"

5 1/4"

4"

61 1/2°

123°

1 5/8"

SHUTTER

4 5/8"
b
(3)
2"
2 1/8" 1/8" STOCK

4"
c
(1)
1 3/4"
1 13/16" 1/4" STOCK

4 3/8"
d
(2)
1 7/8"
2" 1/8" STOCK

10 1/4"

BAY WINDOW DETAILS

1/4"
e
(3)
3 3/16"
2" 1/8"

f
(3)
2"
BEVEL EDGES 61 1/2°
1 7/8" 1/8"

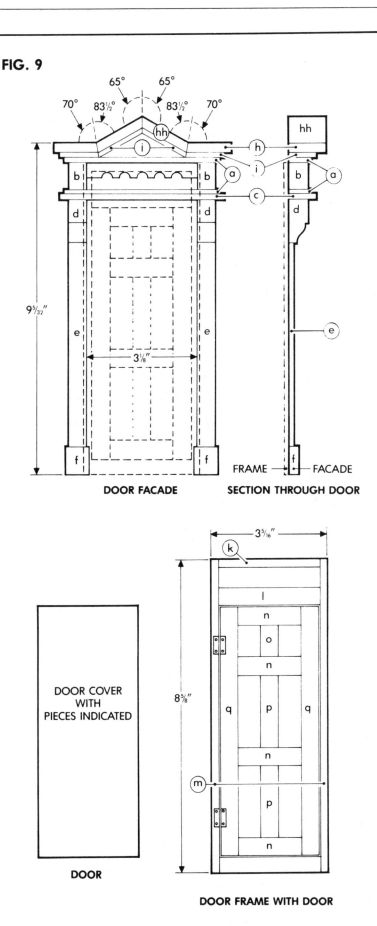

FIG. 9

70° 83½° 65° 65° 83½° 70°

hh

i

b b a a b b

c c

d d d

9⁵/₃₂"

e e e

3⅛"

f f f

DOOR FACADE   **SECTION THROUGH DOOR**

FRAME — FACADE

3⁵/₁₆"

k

l

n

o

n

q p q

8⅝"

n

m

p

n

DOOR COVER
WITH
PIECES INDICATED

DOOR   **DOOR FRAME WITH DOOR**

Toddler Sled

Basically a hand-tool project, this wooden sled is patterned after those made many years ago. It's very practical for toddlers, and the only change that might be required would be the addition of steel strips on the runners if you live in an area of light snowfall.

The back and sides keep the toddler snuggly in place when someone takes the youngster for a ride. An ordinary piece of rope can be used for pulling.

Stock for the sled should be a tough, durable wood such as oak, hickory or ash in at least 1/2 in. net thickness.

The first step is to enlarge the squared drawings and make patterns for the back, sides and runners, and for the front of the sled. Cut all pieces to size and shape. The curves can be cut easily with a coping or jig saw, and by clamping the two sides and two runners together, you will be sure of exact pairs.

Thoroughly sand each piece, then apply several coats of exterior spar or urethane varnish before you assemble the sled. Assemble the sled with brass screws, rather than steel, to avoid rusting. For an added touch, apply decorative decals and coat with varnish. You may not be able to find a brass screweye, so use a zinc or cadmium-plated one to which to tie the tow rope.

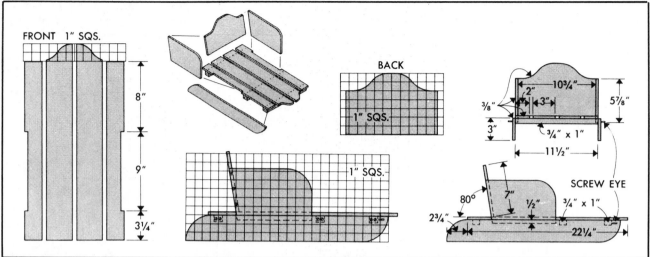

FRONT 1" SQS.

8"

9"

3¼"

BACK

1" SQS.

1" SQS.

10¾"

2"

3"

5⅞"

⅜"

3"

¾" x 1"

11½"

SCREW EYE

¾" x 1"

80°

7"

½"

2¾"

22¼"

Children's Surrey Sled

Pulled by hand or towed behind a garden tractor or a snowmobile, this lightweight sleigh will give youngsters a thrilling ride.

The squared drawing illustrates the compact dimensions on an 18 x 72 in. marine plywood chassis. Using a full 8 ft. length of plywood will permit adding a third seat. The side members are 1 in. pine or redwood (3/4 in. net) for lightness and are assembled with waterproof glue and corrugated fasteners. Glue and screws are used to fasten these assemblies to the plywood floor.

Runners are conventional snow skis, available at sport shops, or you can make your own from 3/8 x 4 in. hickory. Soak or steam the ends for bending, then place them in a form until the wood sets. Trim the blanks to shape after bending. Auto leaf springs, heated and bent to shape, can be used in place of the flat-steel suspensions.

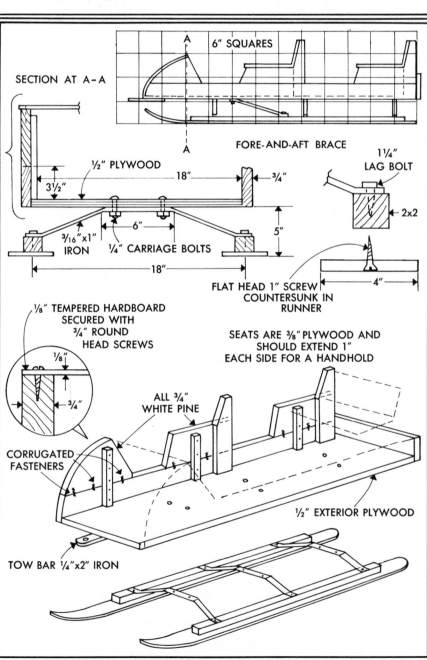

SECTION AT A-A

A

A

6" SQUARES

FORE-AND-AFT BRACE

1¼" LAG BOLT

½" PLYWOOD

18"

¾"

3½"

2x2

³⁄₁₆" x 1" IRON

6"

¼" CARRIAGE BOLTS

5"

18"

FLAT HEAD 1" SCREW COUNTERSUNK IN RUNNER

4"

⅛" TEMPERED HARDBOARD SECURED WITH ¾" ROUND HEAD SCREWS

⅛"

¾"

SEATS ARE ⅜" PLYWOOD AND SHOULD EXTEND 1" EACH SIDE FOR A HANDHOLD

ALL ¾" WHITE PINE

CORRUGATED FASTENERS

½" EXTERIOR PLYWOOD

TOW BAR ¼"x2" IRON

Index